Essentially *Lilly*

a guide to colorful

HOLIDAYS

ALSO BY LILLY PULITZER AND JAY MULVANEY

Essentially Lilly: A Guide to Colorful Entertaining

Essentially Lilly
a guide to colorful
HOLIDAYS

LILLY PULITZER AND JAY MULVANEY

PHOTOGRAPHS BY BEN FINK   ILLUSTRATIONS BY IZAK ZENOU

Collins
An Imprint of HarperCollinsPublishers

ESSENTIALLY LILLY: A GUIDE TO COLORFUL HOLIDAYS.

Copyright © 2005 by Sugartown Worldwide, Inc.

All rights reserved. Printed in China. No part of this book may be used or reproduced in any manner
whatsoever without written permission except in the case of brief quotations embodied in critical articles and reviews.
For information address HarperCollins Publishers, 10 East 53rd Street, New York, NY 10022.

HarperCollins books may be purchased for educational, business, or sales promotional use. For information please write:
Special Markets Department, HarperCollins Publishers, 10 East 53rd Street, New York, NY 10022.

FIRST EDITION

PRODUCED BY 1919 LLC. New York

ART DIRECTION AND DESIGN BY Vertigo Design NYC

ILLUSTRATIONS © 2005 by Izak Zenou. Represented by Traffic NYC

PHOTOGRAPHS © 2005 by Ben Fink, except those listed below

RECIPES © 2005 by Rick Rodgers

Lilly Pulitzer and other Lilly marks are registered trademarks of Sugartown Worldwide, Inc.
All other products referenced in this book are trademarks of their respective companies.

Kate Kuhner, *page 5*
Elizabeth Kuhner, *pages 3 (l), 54 (bottom right), 89 (r), 104 (bottom right)*
From the personal collection of Lilly Pulitzer Rousseau, *pages viii, 2 (l, r), 3 (r), 6, 29 (bottom left),*
54 (except as noted above), 103 (bottom left), 104 (except as noted above), 154, 171 (bottom left)

LIBRARY OF CONGRESS CATALOGING-IN-PUBLICATION DATA HAS BEEN FILED FOR

ISBN 0-06-083244-4

05 06 07 08 09 TP 10 9 8 7 6 5 4 3 2 1

Contents

Lilly circa 1965

An Introduction to Holiday Entertaining
or Let's Tell It Like It Is

I would like to get one or two things straight right off the bat," Lilly tells a friend, in a tone that makes you sit up and listen attentively. "I *despise* the word 'holiday.' I do not like it. Not one iota. It's such a cover-up. If anyone says, 'Happy Holidays' to me, I look them right in the eye and say, 'Merry CHRISTMAS' or 'Happy HANNUKAH' or 'Have a great FOURTH OF JULY.' I love the days; it's just the words—like 'holidays' and 'celebrations'—that I *loathe*. Let's just call them what they are." A Lilly is a Lilly is a Lilly.

Then why a book celebrating holidays? "That is my second point," Lilly adds, slyly revealing that underneath the barefoot casualness of her Palm Beach style is a set of inherent good manners that could teach Emily Post a thing or two. "I have never in my life needed a reason to give a party. They just sort of happen—some with a little bit of planning, some because I want to empty out the icebox and some because people just keep showing up and you can't not feed them. Now, that being said, a few days come around every year that deserve some extra oomph, and that is what this book is all about."

Lilly's life in Palm Beach is centered in her home and revolves around her immediate and extended family, the large circle of close friends who are essentially family and the larger circle of good friends who would be family if there were a banyan gigantic enough to fashion into a family tree. Her "peeps," as she calls them, are woven into the fabric of her life—for example, popping in for some "bakey" (that's bacon) in the morning, coming by for a noontime dip in the pool in an effort to drop a pound or five, bursting through the front door for an after-school Grannie visit or sauntering in at lunchtime on Sunday, knowing they've a standing invitation to come by for a meal prepared by Lilly (and no millionaire on the island can boast a finer cook) and accompanied by lively conversation plus all the island tattle worth knowing.

It's true, then, that every day is a holiday at Lilly's.

LEFT: General Honey and his youth movement *(see page 128)*. Lilly is in top row, far right. RIGHT: Lilly circa 1963.

As for the rest of us—and, in truth, for Lilly as well—there are those traditional days when we honor a variety of occasions—patriotic and religious, sentimental and silly—that strike a deeper emotional chord and deserve to be elevated above the other three-hundred-and-forty-odd days of the year.

The days are traditional, yes, but the way that they're done at Lilly's? Not a chance.

There's an Easter egg hunt every year, followed by lunch for forty, but lunch is served in the slat house, first used to cultivate orchids, and the menu is often grilled hot dogs and cheeseburgers, meatballs from Costco spiced up with a homemade brown sauce and Bananas Foster made with bananas picked from the trees in Lilly's backyard jungle. Thanksgiving is a turkey dinner with all the fixings, but the turkey is cooked a week or two in advance and frozen in its own broth. The invitation to dinner comes with a reminder to bring your bathing suit, as the turkey is served poolside.

Christmas and New Year's tend to merge into an over one-week-long super-holiday, as the Palm Beach contingent—Lilly; daughters Liza and Minnie; son-in-law, Kevin, and grandchildren Bobby, Chris,

LEFT: Lilly and Liza in 1962.
RIGHT: Caca's Macadamia Nuthouse birthday bash featured a hula dance starring (from left to right) Lilly's daughter-in-law Amy, friends Nana and Susanna, son Peter, daughters Liza and Minnie, and grandson Bobby Leidy, in front.

Rodman, Lilly and Jack—is joined by Lilly's son, Peter; his wife, Amy, and their daughters Emma and Charlotte, out from California. By the time you add in cousins and aunts and steps and halfs and exes—all welcomed and warmly embraced—the family has grown into a tribe.

Sometimes the holidays get farmed out; Liza for many years gave a Christmas Eve party and Minnie throws a Fourth of July beach picnic. But there was one yearly celebration that never strayed far from the soul of Lilly's Palm Beach house—the airy slat house that rises out of her beloved jungle of banyans and palms, hardy survivors of hurricane winds (and parties that have packed an almost equal wallop).

"The holiday of the year was always Caca's birthday," Lilly confesses. "Everything else was minor to that." "Caca" was the nickname of Lilly's second husband, the late Enrique Rousseau, a dashing Cuban whose May 31 birthday parties were fantastic expressions of Lilly's imagination, humor and sense of style.

"The plotting and the planning and the phone calls," laughs one of Lilly's closest friends Susanna Cutts. "It would go on for months, and was so much fun."

Every year brought a different theme, with decorations and costumes and skits and songs. Each theme was more elaborate than the last. One year it was the South Seas in the Macadamia Nuthouse; another was Club CacaLoco, when everything was covered in zebra stripes like New York's fabled El Morocco, and life-size wooden cutouts of beauties were mounted around the sides of the slat house. The Under the Sea bash quickly gained notoriety by being called quite something else within the tribe. Also a special favorite was the H. Ross Rousseau for President party, running on the F-lorida A-lternate R-adical T-ycoon ticket.

And each party was as fun and crazy as Lilly's parties can get—"Everybody starts out in the pool and ends up around the piano," Lilly explains.

In addition to Mardi Gras parties, there are Labor Day barbeques, Mother's Day lunches and Christmas Eve caroling parties. There are weekend guest parties and birthday parties for both kids and kids-at-heart. There are boisterous parties on Halloween and a dash of old-fashioned elegance on Valentine's Day. For Lilly, parties come in all shapes and sizes, none favored over the other.

Lilly's recollections of these happy days are vivid snapshots in her memory, bringing forth a smile or, more often, a gutsy laugh as she shares them with her family, close friends and, now, with us. "It's amazing," she says, "when you start picking your life apart and see how much fun you had."

And Lilly continues to have fun, especially at the holidays. So what if these days New Year's Eve is an early-evening champagne party with some cheese and crackers and then, whoosh, everybody out the door by 8:30, en route to their next party, leaving Lilly free to lock her door and turn off the lights. That's Lilly. She doesn't play by the rules.

"Never have," she says with no little pride, "and never will."

Lilly and her "tribe"—kids, grandkids, sister, nieces, cousins, steps, halfs and exes—celebrate the New Year, January 2005.

CLOCKWISE FROM TOP LEFT:

Lilly's parents, Lillian and Robert McKim, ride a tandem bike to a costume parade, Aiken, S.C., 1935.

Little Lilly, with her mother and sisters, riding an elephant at the Westbury Fair in the 1930s.

Lilly with her daughters Minnie and Liza in the mid-1960s.

Lilly on a pony, held by her mother at the Aiken Horseshow, 1935.

Spring

"When I was little I loved to play Pin the Tail on the Donkey, and one April Fool's Day—I must have been four or five—I pinned the donkey's tail to the back of my father's tuxedo before he went out for the evening. I thought it was totally hysterical. I can still see him and mother on that sweeping staircase with that ridiculous tail flapping on his back. He never let on that he knew."

—LILLY

MARDI GRAS

"I went to Mardi Gras once,
for a weekend, and came home
two weeks later."

—LILLY

ardi Gras absolutely lives up to its English translation of Fat Tuesday. It's the last big blow-out before the austere season of Lent begins. It's a time of revelry—a continuous, color-ful and delicious assault on all your senses. Coming six weeks before Easter, Mardi Gras is almost always held in February, which may seem like an odd time in which to welcome in spring.

"What do we care?" asks Lilly, with her customary "who gives a fig" shrug. "It promises that Easter is coming and that spring is on its way. That's reason enough to give a party. Anyway, the Mardi Gras colors are green, purple and gold, and that says spring to me."

Celebrating Mardi Gras has been a New Orleans tradition since 1827. What began as a series of ele-gant masked balls has grown through the decades to become what's called, "The greatest free show on Earth." The Mardi Gras' carnival season starts twelve days after Christmas, on Twelfth Night, January 6, and culminates on the night before Ash Wednesday. The masked balls (many of them much more rowdy than elegant today) are still held every night. Kings and queens reign over their royal courts. Parades are filled with fantastically decorated floats bearing magnificently costumed revelers who respond to the cries of "Throw me somethin', Mister" by tossing doubloons, beads and small trinkets to the festive crowds. Night-time parades are filled with men walking the street carrying flaming torches. Marching bands provide the bouncy soundtrack, and New Orleans laws allowing for the imbibing of all kinds of beverages on public streets undoubtedly add to the fun.

Lilly's first Mardi Gras was a particularly memorable one. "I went to New Orleans for the christening of my goddaughter Lilly Fowler and her twin brother, Paul," she says. "It was being held during Mardi Gras, and I remember thinking, 'How tacky.' But, my Lord, once I saw how great it was, they couldn't get me out of there. I have never seen such a place in my life. So completely wild.

"Mama Paulette had to stay home with the babies, so Papa Bertie and I, along with my great pals Peter and Cheray Duchin, went out every night. The four of us were inseparable. We went to every parade,

Mardi Gras menu

FROZEN HURRICANES

SAZERACS

MINI-CRAB AND CORN CAKES
WITH REMOULADE

SAUSAGE-STUFFED CHICKEN BREASTS
WITH CREOLE SAUCE

RICE AND ARTICHOKE PILAF

KING CAKE

every ball, visited every bar, stood on every balcony. We were literally hanging off the balconies watching the floats go by."

Everyone has lunch parties on their balconies, so you can be there and eat and drink and hang and watch all day long the magical setting of New Orleans, where, as Tennessee Williams said so poetically, "An hour isn't just an hour—but a little piece of eternity dropped into your hands."

"I remember going to one of the queens' balls," Lilly says. "The queen's house was so jam-packed—a real RF (Royal Flush, slang for really crowded). And for some unknown reason I decided that my dress would look better back-to-front. So, I just unzipped it, twisted it around and zipped it back up, right on the dance floor, in the middle of the crowded ballroom. No one even noticed. It was so crazy." Why'd she do it? "The back was cut much lower than the front!"

"We got standing ovations every night as we sauntered into all the seamy French Quarter bars in all our finery," Lilly says. I remember you had to kick mountains of empty beer cans out of the way in order to get from one dive to another. We never went to bed. We slept maybe two hours a night, if that. Every time Bertie and I came home, Mama was standing there, one twin cradled in each arm.

"With glee she would hand them over—one to Bertie, one to me. It could be 5:00 AM or 10:30 AM. It never made any difference. They were always there. Finally, after three mornings of this, I told Paulette that these babies just had to go on a proper schedule. After that, we'd watch the clock before crawling up the stairs.

"When I finally left after two weeks, I got on the bus and slept for twenty-four hours straight, until I reached home. I have never had so much fun in my life."

A Nawlins' native's guide to Mardi Gras

Lilly Fowler Van Gerbig, Lilly's god-daughter, grew up in New Orleans and knows it as only a native can. Here are her tips for an insider's view of the festivities.

Best parades: Number 1 is the Bacchus parade. Close on its heels comes the Zulu, Proteus and Rex (the king of the Rex parade is acknowledged as the king of all Mardi Gras).

Best street to watch from: St. Charles Avenue offers plenty of vantage points and lots of local flavor for parade viewing.

Best restaurants: BEST SEAFOOD: Clancy's, 6100 Annunciation Street; BEST GUMBO: The Gumbo Shop, 630 St. Peter Street; BEST OLD-FASHIONED CREOLE CUISINE: Galatoire's, 209 Bourbon Street; BEST OF THE BEST: Commander's Palace, 1403 Washington Avenue (you'll find tourists there, but it is truly one of the world's outstanding dining experiences).

Best breakfast: Head uptown to the Camellia Grill, 626 South Carrollton Avenue.

Best Hurricanes: Napoleon House Bar & Café, 500 Chartres Street.

Best muffuletta: Napoleon House Bar & Café, 500 Chartres Street.

Best po-boys: Domilise's Po-Boy & Bar, 5240 Annunciation Street, is simply the best in town—"drip down your face good."

Best place to stay: The Columns Hotel on St. Charles Avenue is a charming Victorian mansion turned bed & breakfast.

Best place for music: Storyville District at 125 Bourbon Street is "The Home of Jazz in the Home of Jazz." There is also great music in the heart of the French Quarter at Tipitinas, 501 Napoleon Avenue, and at Lafitte's Blacksmith Shop, 941 Bourbon Street.

Best place to have your palm read: Marie Laveau's House of Voodoo, 739 Bourbon Street.

Mardi Gras throws

Tossing colorful trinkets to the crowds is a time-honored tradition. Strings of beads, doubloons and plastic cups (sassily called New Orleans dinnerware) are thrown from the floats by the costumed and masked revelers.

The most coveted throw of all Mardi Gras is the Zulu Coconut. The Zulu Krewe was the first African-American Krewe, dating back to 1916. Their coconuts, hand-painted and decorated, are real, and still have the milk inside. They are very hard to come by because the supply is limited and they are handed out, not tossed, so you need to be very close to the Zulu float.

A desire for streetcars?

One of the most fun ways to enjoy New Orleans is to ride the city's famous streetcars. Four dollars gets you a day pass on the St. Charles Streetcar—the world's oldest operating street railway—as it ambles past some of the city's most historic landmarks, beautiful gardens and splendid antebellum mansions.

Frozen Hurricanes

All over New Orleans, you'll find bars serving a notoriously potent, fruity drink, The Hurricane, so-called because it's served in a glass shaped like a hurricane gas lamp, and because it will knock you over like a force of nature. Our frozen version is gentler on the system, and every drop as delicious.

FOUR 10-OUNCE DRINKS

> One 12-ounce container frozen mixed fruit punch concentrate
>
> 1½ cups dark rum (this is equal to the amount needed to fill the empty container of fruit punch concentrate)
>
> 1 tray ice cubes (about 16 large ice cubes)
>
> Lime slices, for garnish

Blend together fruit punch concentrate, rum and half of ice cubes until smooth. Add remaining ice cubes and repeat. Pour into tall glasses and garnish with lime slices. Serve immediately.

Sazeracs™

Another classic New Orleans cocktail is the Sazerac. It starts off with a healthy glass of whiskey on the rocks. But it is Peychaud's Bitters (spicier than the typical Angostura™ variety) and Pernod (standing in for the original, and now illegal, ingredient, absinthe, and the hard-to-find Herbsaint) that give the drink distinction.

1 DRINK

> 2 jiggers rye or bourbon whiskey
>
> A splash of anise-flavored liqueur, such as Herbsaint or Pernod™
>
> A few drops of Peychaud's Bitters™ (see Note)
>
> A lemon twist

For each drink, pour whiskey into a cocktail glass filled with ice cubes. Top with liqueur and bitters. Stir and top with lemon twist. Serve chilled.

NOTE: Peychaud's Bitters™ can be mail-ordered from sazerac.com. Or, use Angostura™ bitters, if you wish.

Mini-crab and corn cakes with remoulade

These crab cakes, with sweet nuggets of corn and a crunchy cornmeal crust, will disappear from the platter. Cocktail plates and forks might make them easier to eat, but they're more fun served as finger food.

24 CRAB CAKES

1 pound lump crabmeat, picked over to remove shell and cartilage

1 cup fresh or thawed frozen corn kernels

¼ cup mayonnaise

¼ cup dried bread crumbs

1 large egg, beaten

1 scallion, white and green parts, minced

1 tablespoon Dijon mustard

1 tablespoon Worcestershire sauce

¼ teaspoon hot red pepper sauce

⅔ cup yellow cornmeal

Vegetable oil for frying

Remoulade Sauce (recipe follows)

Combine crabmeat, corn kernels, mayonnaise, bread crumbs, egg, scallion, mustard, Worcestershire sauce and hot red pepper sauce in a large bowl. Let stand for 10 minutes.

Using a tablespoon of mix for each, make 24 plump crab cakes. Spread cornmeal in a shallow dish. Coat crab cakes in cornmeal. Line a baking sheet with waxed paper. Place crab cakes on baking sheet, cover and refrigerate for 30 minutes.

Position rack in center of oven and preheat oven to 200°F. Line another baking sheet with a double thickness of paper towels. Pour enough oil in a large skillet to come ⅛-inch up the sides. Heat on medium-high until the oil is hot and simmering. In batches without crowding, add crab cakes and cook until undersides are golden brown, about 2 minutes. Turn and brown other sides, about 2 minutes more. Transfer to paper towels. If serving immediately, keep warm in oven while making remaining crab cakes. (The crab cakes can be made up to 8 hours ahead, and then cooled, covered and refrigerated. Reheat on a clean baking sheet, loosely covered with aluminum foil, in preheated 350°F oven until heated through, about 7 minutes.)

Top each crab cake with a dab of Remoulade Sauce and serve hot.

REMOULADE SAUCE: Combine ½ cup mayonnaise, 1 chopped scallion (green and white parts), 1 tablespoon finely chopped cornichons (or dill pickles), 1 tablespoon chopped parsley, 1 tablespoon drained, nonpareil capers, 1 teaspoon Dijon mustard, ¼ teaspoon Worcestershire sauce and ¼ teaspoon hot red pepper sauce. Sauce can be made, covered and refrigerated, up to 7 days ahead.

Sausage-stuffed chicken breasts with Creole sauce

Reheated chicken can become tough and dried out. Therefore, chicken dishes can be tricky entrées when you're having a party because they are best when served immediately after cooking. This dish solves the dilemma, baking plump chicken breasts in a make-ahead spicy Creole tomato sauce. 8 SERVINGS

CREOLE SAUCE

2 tablespoons extra-virgin olive oil

1 large onion, chopped

6 scallions, white and green parts, chopped

2 medium celery ribs, chopped

1 large red bell pepper, ribs and seeds removed, chopped

4 garlic cloves, minced

2 tablespoons Cajun seasoning

Two 28-ounce cans crushed tomatoes

One 28-ounce can diced tomatoes in juice

1 pound sweet or hot Italian pork sausage, casings removed

8 chicken breasts with skin and bone, about 14 ounces each

1 teaspoon salt

½ teaspoon freshly ground pepper

Wooden skewers, for closing chicken breasts

Chopped fresh parsley, for garnish

Position rack in center of oven and preheat oven to 400ºF. Lightly oil two 9 X 13-inch baking dishes.

For Creole sauce, heat oil in a large saucepan over medium heat. Add onion, scallions, celery, red pepper and garlic. Cover and cook, stirring occasionally, until vegetables soften, about 10 minutes. Stir in Cajun seasoning, then crushed and diced tomatoes with juice. Bring to a boil. Reduce heat to medium-low and simmer until sauce is lightly thickened, about 30 minutes. (The sauce can be prepared up to 2 days ahead, and then cooled, covered and refrigerated. Reheat before using.)

Remove sausage from casings. Cook in a medium skillet over medium heat, breaking up sausage with a spoon, until cooked through, about 10 minutes. Drain off excess fat. Using a sharp knife, cut deep pocket in thickest part of each breast. Stuff breasts with sausage, and close with wooden skewers.

Spread equal amounts of sauce in baking dishes. Season chicken with salt and pepper. Place 4 breasts in each dish, skin sides up. Bake uncovered until skin is golden brown and an instant-read thermometer inserted in thickest part of breast reads 170ºF, about 40 minutes.

To serve, spoon equal amounts of sauce on 8 dinner plates. Top with chicken breast, garnish with parsley. Serve hot.

Rice and artichoke pilaf

If you struggle with rice dishes, try using converted rice. Much of the rice starch has been removed, so you'll end up with fluffy pilaf and individual grains. Artichoke bottoms, which have a firmer texture than artichoke hearts, give this pilaf Creole flair.

8 SERVINGS

2 tablespoons unsalted butter

½ cup chopped shallots

2 cups long-grain rice, preferably converted

One 14-ounce can artichoke bottoms, drained and cut into bite-size pieces

2 cups chicken broth

½ cup dry white wine, such as Sauvignon Blanc

1¼ teaspoons salt

¼ teaspoon freshly ground pepper

3 tablespoons chopped parsley

Melt butter in a medium saucepan over medium heat. Add shallots and cook, stirring occasionally until softened, about 2 minutes.

Add rice and stir to coat well with butter, about 1 minute. Stir in artichoke bottoms, 2 cups water, chicken broth, wine, salt and pepper. (For even cooking and to avoid overflowing, the ingredients should fill saucepan by no more than one-third. Change pans, if necessary.) Bring to a boil. Cover and reduce heat to low. Let cook until rice is tender and absorbs liquid, about 18 minutes. Let stand 5 minutes. Fluff with a fork and stir in parsley. Transfer to a serving dish and serve hot.

King cake

It isn't Mardi Gras without a king cake, originally presented to the festivities' mock royalty at the end of a ball. A prize in the form of a trinket (such as a porcelain or plastic baby doll, but there are alternatives) is buried in the cake before baking. Tradition dictates that the person who finds the prize in their slice of cake is "King" and either buys the next cake or throws the next party. This sweet yeast dough, filled with a cinnamon pecan swirl and similar to a coffee cake, is not too challenging to make, even for a beginning baker. The purple, green and gold colors on the cake are very important, as they represent the Mardi Gras precepts of justice, faith and power. For the easiest way to get a king cake, try kingcake.com.

10 TO 12 SERVINGS

DOUGH

One ¼-ounce package active dry yeast

¼ cup warm (105 to 115°F) water

¼ cup milk

4 tablespoons (½ stick) unsalted butter, chilled and thinly sliced

¼ cup granulated sugar

Grated zest of 1 orange

1 teaspoon vanilla extract

½ teaspoon freshly grated nutmeg

½ teaspoon salt

1 large egg, beaten

2¾ to 3 cups all-purpose flour

Softened butter, for bowl

FILLING

½ cup pecan halves

⅓ cup packed light brown sugar

2 tablespoons granulated sugar

¾ teaspoon ground cinnamon

1 large egg

Tiny baby doll, clean penny or large dried bean, for the cake

Confectioner's Icing (recipe follows)

Gold-, green- and purple-colored sugar, for decorating (see Note)

To make dough, sprinkle yeast over warm water in a small bowl. Let stand 5 minutes, then stir to dissolve. Bring milk to a boil in a small saucepan. Pour into a mixing bowl of a heavy-duty standing mixer fitted with a paddle blade. Add butter, granulated sugar, orange zest, vanilla, nutmeg and salt. Mix on low speed until butter melts and liquid cools to tepid. Add dissolved yeast and beaten egg. Beat in 1 cup flour and mix until smooth. Add enough flour until dough forms a soft, sticky consistency. Do not add too much flour; dough should not form a ball. Change paddle blade to dough hook and knead on medium speed until dough is smooth and elastic—dough will stick to bowl until end of kneading time.

Butter a medium bowl well. Gather up dough, shape into a ball, place in bowl and turn to coat in butter. Cover tightly in plastic wrap and let stand in warm place until dough doubles in volume (if you stick a finger into the dough, it will leave an impression), about 1 hour. Punch down dough to deflate.

To make filling, grind pecans with brown sugar, granulated sugar and cinnamon in a food processor or blender. Beat egg in a small bowl. On a lightly floured surface, pat out dough into a rectangle. Dust top with flour and roll out into 18 X 8-inch rectangle. Brush with beaten egg. Leaving 1-inch border, sprinkle with pecan sugar, and randomly place the doll or other object on the sugar. Starting at long end, roll up into a cylinder; pinch long seam closed. Transfer to parchment

paper–lined baking sheet, seam side down. Form dough into a ring, tucking one end of dough into the other to close ring; brush inside of seam with egg and pinch closed. Cover loosely with plastic wrap and let stand in warm place until almost doubled, about 30 minutes.

Position rack in center of oven and preheat oven to 350°F. Pierce top of cake in a few places with tip of knife and brush with beaten egg. Bake until cake is golden brown and bottom sounds hollow when rapped with knuckles, 30 to 35 minutes. Cool completely on wire cake rack.

Place cake on wire cake rack over baking sheet. Spread about two-thirds icing over cake. Decorate with splotches of col-

ored sugar (do not mix colors). Drizzle remaining icing over cake. Let stand to set icing. Cut into wedges to serve. (The cake is best the day it is baked. You can also freeze the undecorated cake, wrapped in plastic wrap and aluminum foil, for up to 1 month. The day of serving, thaw cake at room temperature, then decorate with icing and sugars.)

CONFECTIONER'S ICING: Sift 2 cups confectioner's sugar into a medium bowl. Gradually whisk in enough water (about 3 tablespoons) until icing is consistency of thick heavy cream.

NOTE: Colored sugars are available at cake decorating supply stores, and by mail order from KitchenKraft.com and patsbulkfood.com.

EASTER

"Here comes Peter Cottontail,
hoppin' down the bunny trail..."

—A FAVORITE CHILDHOOD
DIITY OF LILLY'S

Not every hostess prepares Easter dinner by pouring a can of soda pop on the main course and plopping it in the oven while she goes out and joins the party. Nor is it every household where a young lady in a bathing suit and a pair of pink fuzzy ears hands you your beverage of choice while executing a "Playboy Bunny Dip." But that's Lilly—no, not handing out the drinks, but being relaxed about the whole enchilada and having fun. (It was her friend Nancy Kezele, called "Na-Na"—accent on the second syllable—who perfected the bunny dip—that "dip, twist and serve-a-drink" move.)

"I'm not into major planning," Lilly explains. "We take the eggs and the bunny decorations out of storage a day or two before Easter and then just pull it together."

"Think about it. Do it. Get on with it." Simple rules, and about as much advice as you'll get from Lilly on the "art" or "philosophy" of entertaining before she sniggers at you and tosses a cushion at your swelled head with spot-on accuracy.

And as for the ham cooked in soda pop? "Well, you've got to keep the ham a little wet…I buy a spiral-cut ham, pour some ginger ale or Coca-Cola and pineapple juice over it, cover it in foil and toss it in the oven. Couldn't be easier. Stick in all those cloves? Oh, I'd just end up choking on them. Pineapple rings with cherries in the center? Not for me. I just want to have a good piece of ham."

These days Easter alternates between Lilly's house and her sister Flo's just down the road. It's not unusual for the celebrations to draw together close to forty people, with the customary "FCFOS" blend of family, close friends, orphans and strays (orphans are the regulars who have no place to go on holidays, strays are the visiting firemen under the same circumstances).

There used to be even more folks when Lilly lived over on Lake Worth. "We'd give Easter parties and have this huge snake of tables out on the lawn, each one covered in brightly patterned fabric, nothing matching of course. We'd hang big colorful umbrellas up in the trees. Everyone in their bonnets, all those eggs—and we would boil hundreds of eggs. It was always very pretty.

Easter menu

LATINO SHRIMP AND CORN BISQUE

BAKED HAM WITH GINGER-PINEAPPLE GLAZE

CREAMED EGG GRATIN

BAKER-STYLE YUKON GOLD POTATOES AND LEEKS

ASPARAGUS WITH TOASTED ALMONDS AND GARLIC

FROZEN SHERBET CAKE WITH PECAN CRUST

"We'd end up on top of the tables after lunch with our own Easter parade, modeling our hats," Lilly remembers with a laugh.

"What you have to understand about Lilly's," says her pal Susanna Cutts, "is that you never know what's going to happen when you walk through the door. It could be five people or fifty. One Easter Lilly was there plunking hats on everyone's head as we came into the house. Floppy hats, straw hats, baseball caps—it didn't matter. Everyone got a hat and we had our bonnet parade."

An Easter Bonnet Tabletop Parade isn't the only tradition carried out in an untraditional style. There's the annual Easter egg hunt, of course, but the eggs are hidden in Lilly's dense, tropical jungle. The

little egg hunters turn into a troop of explorers, all in search of the golden egg. Or, failing that, the silver or even the metallic pink egg. Those three are prized among the dozens of others, and so highly sought after that a sharp elbow is sometimes brought into use. The reason is because they are filled not with candy, but with a different kind of treat—the green folding papery kind.

"The big kids just toss the smaller ones out of the way," laughs Lilly, but her keen eye makes sure that everyone gets a fair shake at the bounty. In addition to the big prize eggs, there are dozens of plastic eggs filled with coins, chewing gum, candy and "dead bugs or whatever else we can cram in!" adds Lilly, as well as lots and lots of gaily decorated hard-boiled eggs.

Spending the Saturday afternoon before Easter preparing the eggs was a preholiday ritual in Lilly's house. "We would set up operations out in the slat house," remembers her daughter Liza. "Out came tons of hard-boiled eggs and cups and cups of colored dye. Nieces, nephews, cousins, neighbors, friends, a whole slew of kids would come over to decorate. We'd use Magic Marker and crayons. It seemed like there were always hundreds of Easter eggs."

"Needless to say," adds Lilly, "smelly eggs would be found in the jungle for the next six months. But it was fun. We'd do some slightly risqué ones for the adults and use them as place cards on the tables. People would look at them and do the biggest double takes."

"Irreverence is the key to every event at Lilly's," explains Na-Na. "Things just unfold."

And sometimes even the best-laid plans went a little astray. One long ago Easter, Lilly's former son-in-law Bob Leidy came dressed up as the Easter Bunny, "with the ears and the mask and the perfect bunny suit and basket," Liza explains. "He was sweating and miserable. Our son Bobby was so excited and happy and then he looked down and saw Bob's shoes. Bob couldn't fit into the bunny slippers, so he wore his own shoes. Bobby looked up at the bunny, looked at me and then started wailing, 'Look, the Easter Bunny has stolen daddy's shoes. We laughed for days."

One sure way to calm a wailing grandson and the perfect way to top an Easter lunch is Lilly's favorite dessert: a Carvel Easter Bunny ice cream cake. An odd choice for the Queen of Palm Beach? "Who else makes one?" Lilly asks. "No one I know of, and I'm not gonna do it!

"Besides that, it's de-lish," she adds.

Has anyone seen Elmer Fudd?

"One year those *awful* girls from my shop gave me a pair of little bunnies— two of the opposite sex. I set them to live in my beautiful walled garden off my bedroom, which had an outdoor sauna and $3,500 of new landscaping. You can guess what happened. Within two seconds there were sixty bunnies hopping around. It's true; it was like that commercial when the guy is waiting for his credit card in the pet shop and the bunnies keep coming and coming and coming. They ate everything in my garden, and they ruined the sauna.

Needless to say, there was a big bunny sale on our street. I didn't care whose pot they ended up in!"

—Lilly's "favorite" Easter

Easter egg decorating

You start with hard-boiled eggs. Lilly used to boil "hundreds" of them; these days she's down to "dozens." Then you mix cups of dye—food dye, Easter Egg coloring mix, food coloring—in as many colors as you can find.

Before you dip the eggs, wrap rubber bands around them, or color designs with wax crayons, which will resist the dye.

After you've dyed the eggs, go to town with markers, colored pencils, glitter pens, thin ribbons and glue. Lilly uses a black Sharpie to create abstract designs on her eggs that she then colors in with the brightest colors available.

Go crazy! Make portrait eggs, paisley eggs, Lilly eggs—just make sure you use lots of color and have lots of fun.

Easter movies

Easter is the appropriate holiday for all of those extravagant Hollywood Biblical epics from the 1950s and 60s— THE ROBE, BEN-HUR, KING OF KINGS, THE GREATEST STORY EVER TOLD. But, for some lighter fare, why not go back a few more years in Hollywood's history to the classic EASTER PARADE. As someone once said, "It's not exactly a religious experience, but with Fred Astaire, Judy Garland, Ann Miller, Peter Lawford and music by Irving Berlin, it's almost as good."

Latino shrimp and corn bisque

Soup is a perfect first course for a big meal because it can be made ahead of time and reheated just before serving, giving a break to the busy cook. This lovely soup is quite easy to make. 8 SERVINGS

1½ pounds medium (26 to 30 count) shrimp

3 cups bottled clam juice

2 sprigs fresh parsley

⅛ teaspoon dried thyme

⅛ teaspoon whole black peppercorns

5 tablespoons (½ stick plus 1 tablespoon) unsalted butter

1 medium onion, finely chopped

1 small celery rib with leaves, finely chopped

½ cup diced (¼-inch) chopped red bell pepper

2 garlic cloves, minced

⅓ cup all-purpose flour

¼ cup dry sherry

1 tablespoon tomato paste

1½ cups fresh or frozen corn kernels

½ cup heavy cream, plus additional for garnish, if desired

Salt and freshly ground pepper, to taste

Chopped fresh cilantro, for garnish

Peel and devein shrimp, reserving shells. Coarsely chop shrimp, and then cover and refrigerate. Bring shrimp shells, 1 quart water, clam juice, parsley, thyme and peppercorns to a boil in a medium saucepan over high heat. Reduce heat to low and simmer for 30 minutes to blend flavors. Strain and reserve liquid.

Melt butter in a large saucepan over medium-low heat. Add onion, celery, red pepper and garlic, and then cover. Cook until vegetables soften, about 3 minutes. Sprinkle with flour and stir well. Whisk in reserved cooking liquid, sherry and tomato paste. Bring to a simmer over medium heat. Reduce heat to low and cook until lightly thickened, about 3 minutes. (The soup can be prepared up to this point 1 day ahead, and then cooled, covered and refrigerated. Reheat to simmering over low heat.) Stir in reserved shrimp, corn and heavy cream and cook just until the shrimp turn opaque, about 3 minutes. Season with salt and pepper. Transfer soup to a warm soup tureen.

To serve, ladle the soup into bowls. Top each serving with a drizzle of cream, if desired, and sprinkle with cilantro. Serve hot.

Baked ham with ginger-pineapple glaze

Lilly invented this recipe on the spot one day when she went to the icebox looking for a Coke™ to splash on her ham, only to find nothing but a can of ginger ale.

Spiral-sliced hams are easy to find at supermarkets and price clubs, and they are certainly easy to carve. The sweet, fruity pineapple topping is just what everyone really wants in a ham. The glaze's rate of evaporation depends on the size of your roasting pan—you may not need to add more ginger ale as the ham cooks, or you just might. 12 SERVINGS

One 20-ounce can crushed pineapple in juice, well drained, juices reserved

Two 12-ounce cans ginger ale, as needed

1 cup packed light brown sugar

1 tablespoon dry mustard

One 8-pound spiral-sliced smoked ham

Position rack in center of oven and preheat to 325°F. Oil a large roasting pan.

Mix pineapple juice, 1 can (12 ounces) ginger ale, brown sugar and mustard in a blender to dissolve mustard. Set aside.

Place ham, flat side down, in the pan. Pour pineapple juice mixture over the ham. Pat the crushed pineapple onto the ham; if you press hard, it will stick nicely. Place pan with ham and pineapple juice on top of stove and bring to a boil over two burners on high heat. Tent ham with foil and transfer to oven.

Bake for 1 hour, checking occasionally to be sure that juices aren't burning and adding a bit more ginger ale to the pan if needed to keep the juices moist. Discard foil tent, and baste ham with pan juices. Bake, basting occasionally and adding more ginger ale to pan if needed, until a meat thermometer inserted halfway into ham, but not touching the bone, reads 140°F, about 45 minutes more. Transfer ham to a serving platter and tent with foil to keep warm. Let the ham stand for 15 minutes.

Meanwhile, place roasting pan over two burners on high heat and bring juices to a boil. Cook, stirring occasionally, until juices are dark and syrupy, 5 to 10 minutes. Pour juices over ham and serve.

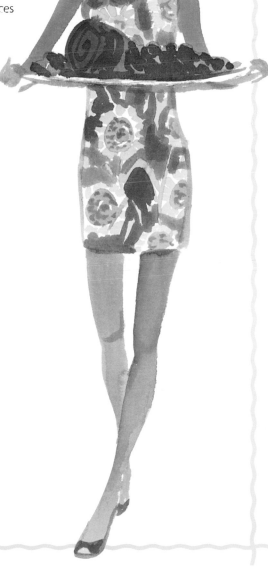

Creamed egg gratin

At Easter, eggs should be featured in the menu. Here's an old-fashioned dish Lilly and her sister Flo loved growing up, with quartered hard-boiled eggs smothered in lots of cheddar cheese sauce. 8 TO 12 SERVINGS

1 dozen large eggs

6 tablespoons unsalted butter, divided

1 medium onion, finely chopped

1½ cups milk

1 cup chicken broth

⅓ cup all-purpose flour

1 cup (4 ounces) shredded extra-sharp Cheddar cheese, divided

1 tablespoon Dijon mustard

Salt and freshly ground pepper, to taste

¼ cup freshly grated Parmesan cheese

Place eggs in a medium saucepan just large enough to hold eggs in a single layer. Add cold water to cover. Bring water just to a boil over high heat. Reduce heat to medium-low and simmer for 1 minute. Remove pan from heat and cover tightly. Let eggs stand in saucepan for 15 minutes. Drain and transfer to a bowl of very cold water. Cool completely. Crack eggs and remove shells. Cut each egg lengthwise into quarters. Save 2 egg quarters, for garnish.

Position rack in center of oven and preheat to 350ºF. Butter a 9 X 13-inch baking dish.

Melt 2 tablespoons butter in a medium saucepan over medium heat. Add onion and cover. Cook, stirring often, until golden brown, about 10 minutes. Meanwhile, combine milk and broth in a small saucepan and heat to simmering over medium heat (or combine in a large measuring cup and heat in a microwave oven). Add 3 more tablespoons butter to onions and melt. Sprinkle with flour and stir well. Whisk in hot milk mixture, and cook, whisking often, until simmer-ing and thickened, about 3 minutes. Stir in ½ cup Cheddar cheese and mustard. Season with salt and pepper.

Arrange quartered eggs, smooth sides down, in baking dish. Pour sauce over eggs. Sprinkle with remaining ½ cup Cheddar cheese and the Parmesan. Cut remaining 1 table-spoon butter into small cubes and dot cheese with butter cubes. (The eggs can be prepared 1 day ahead, and then cooled, covered and refrigerated.)

Bake until sauce is bubbling throughout, about 35 minutes. Finely chop reserved egg quarters, and sprinkle over gratin. Serve hot.

Baker-style Yukon Gold potatoes and leeks

These delicious potatoes may not be the prettiest thing to ever come out of Lilly's kitchen, but they taste great, especially in tandem with the rich ham and creamed eggs. 8 SERVINGS

10 tablespoons unsalted butter, divided

6 large leeks, white and pale green part only, thinly sliced, well rinsed and drained (6 cups)

5 pounds Yukon Gold potatoes

1½ teaspoons salt

½ teaspoon freshly ground pepper

2 cups chicken broth

1 cup dry white wine

2 tablespoons chopped fresh parsley, for garnish

Position rack in center of oven and preheat to 350ºF. Butter a 10 X 15-inch baking dish.

Melt 2 tablespoons butter in a large skillet over medium heat. Add leeks and cover. Cook, stirring often, until tender, about 10 minutes.

Meanwhile, peel potatoes. Using a food processor fitted with the slicing blade or a mandoline, slice potatoes into ⅛-inch-thick rounds. Do not immerse the potatoes in water to keep them from turning brown. You want them to retain their starch, which helps the slices stick together and makes for easier serving. Move quickly, so they won't discolor.

Mix salt and pepper together. Layer half of potatoes, leeks and remaining potatoes in baking dish, seasoning layers with salt and pepper. Bring broth, wine and remaining butter in a medium saucepan to a boil over high heat, and pour over potatoes. Cover tightly with aluminum foil.

Bake for 1 hour. Uncover and bake until the juices are thick and bubbling and the potatoes are tender when pierced with a knife, about 30 minutes more. (The potatoes can be baked 1 day ahead, cooled, covered with foil, and refrigerated. Just before reheating, pour ½ cup chicken broth over potatoes. Bake in a preheated 350°F oven until heated through, about 30 minutes.) Let stand 5 minutes. Sprinkle with parsley and serve hot.

Asparagus with toasted almonds and garlic

Easter is all about the arrival of spring, and asparagus is about as "spring" as you can get. This is a fine way to make asparagus special, with the crunch of toasted almonds and a good amount of garlic. 8 SERVINGS

3 pounds asparagus

½ cup sliced natural or blanched almonds

2 tablespoons olive oil

2 garlic cloves, finely chopped

Salt and freshly ground pepper, to taste

Bring a large pot of lightly salted water to a boil over high heat. Snap off and discard woody ends of asparagus where they meet the more tender flesh. Cut trimmed asparagus spears on diagonal into 2-inch-long pieces. Cook asparagus in boiling water until crisp-tender, about 4 minutes, depending on thickness of asparagus. Drain, rinse under cold water and drain again. Pat asparagus dry with paper towels. (The asparagus can be prepared up to 1 day ahead, and then wrapped in dry paper towels, stored in plastic bags and refrigerated.)

Heat a large skillet over medium heat. Add almonds and cook, stirring occasionally, until toasted, about 3 minutes. Transfer to a plate. (The almonds can be prepared up to 1 day ahead, covered tightly and stored at room temperature.)

Heat oil and garlic together in a large skillet over medium heat until garlic begins to color, about 2 minutes. Add asparagus and cook, stirring often, until heated through, about 5 minutes. Stir in almonds. Season with salt and pepper. Transfer to a serving dish and serve hot.

Frozen sherbet cake with pecan crust

You can substitute your favorite sherbet or sorbet flavor for the raspberry and lemon here. Try tropical flavors, like mango, lime or even coconut. Or, do an all-citrus cake with lemon and orange. Use slices of fresh fruit to garnish. 8 TO 10 SERVINGS

CRUST

⅔ cup vanilla wafer cookie crumbs (crushed)

⅓ cup chopped pecans

2 tablespoons granulated sugar

2 tablespoons unsalted butter, melted

FILLING

1 quart lemon sherbet

1 quart raspberry sherbet

½ cup heavy cream

2 tablespoons confectioner's sugar

½ teaspoon vanilla extract

Fresh raspberries and mint sprigs, for garnish

Raspberry Sauce (recipe follows)

Position rack in center of oven and preheat to 350°F. Lightly butter a 9 X 3-inch springform pan.

To make pecan crust, process cookie crumbs, pecans and sugar in a food processor or blender until pecans are very finely chopped. Transfer to a bowl, then add butter and stir until crumbs are evenly moistened. Press evenly into bottom and ½ inch up sides of pan. Bake until lightly browned, about 10 minutes. Cool completely on a wire cake rack.

Soften lemon sherbet by placing in a bowl and mashing with a large rubber spatula. Spread evenly in cooled crust. Cover with plastic wrap and freeze until firmed, about 20 minutes. Soften raspberry sherbet in the same manner and spread over lemon sherbet. Cover with plastic wrap, pressing wrap directly on sherbet, and freeze until firm, at least 4 hours. (The cake can be prepared up to this point 1 day ahead.)

When ready to serve, whip heavy cream, confectioner's sugar and vanilla in a medium bowl with an electric mixer on high speed until stiff. Transfer to a pastry bag fitted with a large star tip. Remove plastic wrap from cake. Pipe 12 rosettes around edge of cake, and garnish with raspberries and mint. Slice with a warm (dip in a glass of hot water) thin knife. Serve frozen, with Raspberry Sauce.

RASPBERRY SAUCE: Purée 1 pint raspberries, ⅓ cup granulated sugar and 1 teaspoon fresh lemon juice in a food processor. Taste. Add sugar and lemon juice as needed, and blend again to dissolve sugar. Strain through fine wire sieve into a bowl. Cover and refrigerate until chilled, about 1 hour. (The sauce can be made 1 day ahead, and then covered and refrigerated.)

MOTHER'S DAY

"Mom has an amazing zest for life.
It's like a big hug."

—LILLY'S SON PETER

other's Day was not such a big thing when I was growing up," recalls Lilly, "though I do remember that I used to run outside and search for lilies of the valley, hoping they were still in bloom. I would gather up a bunch of them and make a small bouquet by wrapping a paper doily around them, then presenting them to my mum before running off to play."

"Mum" was the estimable Lillian Bostwick McKim Phipps, who raised Lilly, a brunette, and her sisters Memsie, a blonde, and Flossie, a raging redhead (formally called Lillian Lee, Marie Maud and Florence Fitch) in a manner completely different from the casual, laid-back life that Lilly leads today in Palm Beach. Lilly's childhood was spent in New York—winters in the city, summers on Long Island. Long Island meant an estate in Roslyn, and in New York City, home was a large limestone house at 4 East 79th Street, a few steps from Central Park. As Lilly remembers, "It was so beautiful; up on the top, top floor there was this glass room that we used as a play room. And it was a proper house."

In the language of the time, a "proper house" meant a house that was properly staffed, and the Phipps' house was surely that. There were two or three servants in the kitchen, two servants in the pantry, a butler, a footman, housemaids, a lady's maid for madam, a mademoiselle for the girls, a Scottish nanny for the two younger ones, a chauffeur and then help down in the laundry. Phew!

"It was so formal," Lilly remembers. "Mother would sit in her bed, and every morning the red menu book would come in on her tray and the meals would be planned—luncheons, dinners, kids' suppers, the works—and a guesstimate of how many for what meal. In the summer there were seven of us kids, plus three nannies and, of course, each of us had a dog.

"Mother always had the most incredible teas, every afternoon at 4:45," adds Lilly. "People dropped in out of the woodwork for her teas. The butler set up the tea table in grand style with Mme Porthault's lovely bové linens. A cake, fresh out of the oven every day, with icing dripping down the sides was served, along with little sandwiches, scones, cookies and hot cinnamon toast. Mother served hot tea in the winter and iced tea in the summer. We would all huddle to pounce on all the goodies.

The luncheon

WHITE SANGRIA WITH ORANGES AND RASPBERRIES

BEEF AND OLIVE EMPANADAS

SEAFOOD AND AVOCADO SALAD WITH LIME VINAIGRETTE

FRESH BAKED ROLLS

TOASTED COCONUT FLAN

"Sometimes on Mother's Day we would recite poems or sing. Once I took a record of my step-father's and learned all the words. I got up to sing along with the record. I couldn't have been more than six or seven, so of course I had no idea what the words meant. Well, by the time I got to the chorus, there was such an uproar as you have ever seen. They almost died. They yanked the record off and disappeared out of the room with it."

And the song that caused this riotous laughter?

Lilly clears her throat and sings a line or two. "'There's a pet I love to pet. Every evening we get set. I stroke it every chance I get…' Well, that's as far as I'll go only to say it's a song about a girl and her kitty cat and it's meant for a gentleman's ears only. No wonder they were collapsing. Can you imagine that song coming from sweet little me?"

For a "sweet little" gal who once confessed that there was someone to tie her shoes for her until she was twelve, it boggles the mind that Lilly can, by herself, turn out dinner for thirty without batting an eye. But that's what's so great about her credo: Always look forward, rarely look back.

Nowadays Mother's Day at Lilly's is likely to be a low-key but very happy affair—a dinner or lunch with family (always Minnie and Liza and kids if they're in town; Peter's always in California) and a few close friends—that is, if she even remembers. "Lilly forgets Mother's Day just about every year," snitches her pal Mark Gilbertson. But it's more a case that people love her so much that they don't need to wait until the second Sunday in May to express it.

A recent Mother's Day nicely demonstrates Lilly's theory of the five "Fs" of entertaining: Family, Friends, Flowers, Food and Fun. A buffet supper with a Latin-flavored menu was planned in the slat house and that afternoon two long tables were set with brightly colored tablecloths, place mats and napkins. A row of pottery vases, each holding two or three vividly red and orange Gerber daisies, ran down the length of the tables. Photographic equipment was strewn about, as Lilly was being photographed for a magazine story. Liza and a friend were recruited to assist the photographer by holding up light filters, which they did while teetering on boxes and stools. After an hour in the hot sun, the photo shoot ended and as the photographer and his assistant were packing up, Lilly turned to them and said, "All-righty-roo, dinner is at 8:00, so we'll see you back here then." It's like that at Lilly's. Walk through the door and you're a friend. Stay for an hour and you're part of the family.

That night the slat house overflowed with Lilly lovers of all shapes, sizes and relations: children, grandchildren, siblings and friends old and, as of that afternoon, brand new. Candlelight, a sumptuous buffet ("She gives new meaning to the term 'groaning board,'" says her friend Eloise Cuddeback) and the sound of continuous laughter filled the spring night. Then came the toasts. Her daughters spoke lovingly, as did her oldest grandson. Then a friend stood, tapped his glass and read aloud from a letter John Kenneth Galbraith, the eminent economist and former ambassador to India, had written forty years earlier, describing a dinner given in his honor in 1962 at the White House. Galbraith enjoyed the evening and made particular mention of his dinner partner. "Lilly Pulitzer, she of the Palm Beach tan and admirable shape." With that the slat house erupted in laughter and a salute rang out to "Lilly and her still quite admirable shape."

Top ten movie moms

1. Irene Dunne • *I Remember Mama*
2. Shirley MacLaine • *Terms of Endearment*
3. Debra Winger • *Terms of Endearment*
4. Diane Keaton • *Baby Boom*
5. Barbara Stanwyck • *Stella Dallas*
6. Jamie Lee Curtis • *Freaky Friday*
7. Julia Roberts • *Stepmom*
8. Olympia Dukakis • *Moonstruck*
9. Lana Turner • *Imitation of Life*
10. Anjelica Huston • *Addams Family Values*

Nowhere in the running:

1. Faye Dunaway • *Mommie Dearest*
2. Rosalind Russell • *Gypsy*
3. Anne Ramsey • *Throw Momma from the Train*

Lilly remembers when:

We all smoked and/or drank, took aspirin, ate blue cheese dressing and didn't get tested for diabetes while carrying the little darlings.

We painted their cribs with bright lead-based paints.

There were no childproof lids on medicine bottles, doors or cabinets.

There were also no bike helmets, seat-belts or airbags.

The kids would leave home in the morning and play all day, as long as they were back when the streetlights came on.

There were no PlayStations, video games, cable TV, cell phones or internet chat rooms…there were friends and we went outside and played with them.

We ate cupcakes, bread and butter and drank soda pop with sugar, but we weren't overweight because we were always outside playing.

We fell out of trees, got cut and broke bones and teeth, and there were no lawsuits from these accidents.

We made up games with sticks and tennis balls and although we were told it would happen, we did not put out very many eyes.

We had freedom, failure, success and responsibility, and learned how to deal with it all.

Ah, the good old days.

The mommy project

Few things are as special, and as cherished, as a gift that is made with love. Think about that for Mother's Day. If you can knit, knit. If you can sew, sew. If baking's your thing, head to the kitchen. And if all else fails, everyone can glue!

Take a box or a picture frame or a mirror, and make it uniquely Mom's. Take some glue and some things to glue on—bits of costume jewelry, pretty seashells, a marble or two—and you're set to go!

White sangría with oranges and raspberries

Sangría made with red wine is well known, but this cool and refreshing white wine version deserves equal attention. It's flavored with orange liqueur; while clear Triple Sec will do, Cognac-based Grand Marnier has a deeper flavor. Make sangría a day before brunch so flavors have time to blend. 8 SERVINGS

One 750-ml bottle dry white wine, such as Sauvignon Blanc

$\frac{1}{2}$ cup orange-flavored liqueur, preferably Grand Marnier

2 cups red or green seedless grapes, cut in halves lengthwise

$\frac{1}{2}$ pint raspberries

Orange slices, for garnish

Mix wine, liqueur, grapes and raspberries in a large covered container or nonreactive bowl. Cover and refrigerate until well chilled, at least 6 hours or preferably overnight.

To serve, divide sangría and fruit between wine glasses. Garnish with orange slices. Serve chilled.

Beef and olive empanadas

One of Latin cuisine's most famous dishes, these mildly spiced, flaky meat pies are a great appetizer to feed your guests as they arrive. You can bake them a day or two ahead of time, and warm them up in the oven for serving. 18 EMPANADAS

FILLING

1 tablespoon olive oil

1 small onion, finely chopped

1 garlic clove, minced

$\frac{1}{2}$ pound ground round

$\frac{1}{2}$ teaspoon ground cumin

$\frac{1}{2}$ teaspoon dried oregano

$\frac{1}{8}$ teaspoon ground cinnamon

$\frac{1}{8}$ teaspoon crushed hot red pepper

$\frac{1}{2}$ cup tomato sauce

$\frac{1}{3}$ cup coarsely chopped pimento-stuffed green olives

3 tablespoons golden or dark raisins

Salt, to taste

$1\frac{1}{2}$ (3 sheets) 17-ounce packages puff pastry sheets, thawed overnight in refrigerator

1 large egg, beaten, for glaze

To make filling, heat oil in a medium skillet over medium heat. Add onion and garlic. Cook, stirring often, until onion softens, about 3 minutes. Add ground round and cook, breaking up meat with a spoon, until it loses its raw color, about 5 minutes. Drain off any fat that has accumulated. Stir in ground cumin, oregano, cinnamon and crushed red pepper. Add tomato sauce, olives and raisins, and mix. Bring to a simmer and reduce heat to medium-low. Cook until filling is thickened, about 15 minutes. Season with salt. Cool completely.

Position rack in center of oven and preheat oven to 400°F. Working with 1 puff pastry sheet at a time, place pastry on a lightly floured work surface. Dust top with flour and roll pastry out to a 12 X 9-inch sheet. Using a 4-inch-diameter cookie cutter or saucer, cut out 6 rounds. Brush edge of a round with beaten egg. Place about 1 tablespoon filling on pastry round,

fold in half to enclose filling and press edges closed with a fork. Place on a baking sheet. Repeat with remaining rounds and filling. Brush tops of empanadas with beaten egg.

Bake until empanadas are golden brown, about 20 minutes. Cool slightly, and serve warm. (The empanadas can be made 1 day ahead, and then cooled completely, wrapped tightly in aluminum foil and refrigerated. Reheat on a baking sheet, tented with foil, in a preheated 350°F oven until cooked through, about 15 minutes.)

Seafood and avocado salad with lime vinaigrette

Lobster and crab may be elegant, but they are pricey. Mussels (in or out of the shell), grilled diced swordfish or cooked calamari could be added to or substituted for the seafood listed in the recipe. The acids in the lime vinaigrette will help keep the avocados from turning brown, so you can make the salad a few hours ahead of time without concern. 8 SERVINGS

SEAFOOD

1 cup dry white wine

1 small onion, sliced

¼ teaspoon dried thyme

¾ teaspoon salt

¼ teaspoon whole black peppercorns

1½ pounds bay scallops

1 pound large (21 to 25 count) shrimp, peeled and deveined

1 pound lobster or crabmeat

2 ripe Florida (or 3 Hass) avocados, pitted, peeled and cut into ¾-inch cubes

1 pint grape tomatoes, cut lengthwise into halves

2 scallions, white and green parts, finely chopped

1 jalapeño, seeded and minced

1 large head green leaf lettuce, separated into individual leaves, washed and dried

Lime Vinaigrette (recipe follows)

To prepare seafood, bring 2 quarts water, wine, onion, thyme, salt and peppercorns to a boil over high heat in a large non-reactive (stainless steel) saucepan. Add scallops and cook just until they turn opaque, about 3 minutes. Using a large skimmer or wire strainer, transfer scallops to a rimmed baking sheet. Add shrimp to same liquid, and cook until they turn opaque, about 3 minutes. Transfer shrimp to baking sheet. Cool completely. Cut shrimp in halves lengthwise. Cover and refrigerate until seafood is chilled, at least 2 hours. (The seafood can be prepared 1 day ahead, and then covered and refrigerated.)

Check lobster or crabmeat for pieces of shell or cartilage, and cut into bite-size pieces. Combine lobster or crabmeat, avocados, tomatoes, scallions and jalapeño in a large glass, ceramic or stainless steel bowl. Drizzle with ⅓ cup Lime Vinaigrette, and mix gently. (The salad can be prepared up to 4 hours ahead, and then covered tightly with plastic wrap and refrigerated.)

Line a large platter with lettuce leaves. Heap salad in center of platter. Drizzle a few tablespoons of Lime Vinaigrette over lettuce, and pour remaining Lime Vinaigrette into a small sauceboat. Serve salad chilled, with Lime Vinaigrette passed on side.

LIME VINAIGRETTE: In a medium bowl, whisk together grated zest of 2 limes, 6 tablespoons fresh lime juice and 1 garlic clove, crushed and peeled. Gradually whisk in 1⅓ cups extra-virgin olive oil, then 2 tablespoons minced shallot. Season with salt and pepper to taste. (The vinaigrette can be prepared 1 day ahead, and then covered and refrigerated. If vinaigrette separates, whisk well to recombine.)

Toasted coconut flan

Smooth as silk, these custards are full of coconut flavor. There is a special, easy manual technique to removing flans from their ramekins; do not use a knife to release the custard, or you'll cut it, leaving little flecks of custard in the caramel syrup. You'll need eight 6-ounce ramekins or custard cups to make the flans. 8 SERVINGS

2 cups sugar, divided

2½ cups canned coconut milk (shake well before measuring)

6 large eggs, plus 3 large yolks

1 teaspoon vanilla

½ cup sweetened coconut flakes, toasted (see Note)

Position rack in center of oven and preheat to 325°F. Lightly butter 6-ounce ramekins or custard cups.

Bring 1¼ cups sugar and ¼ cup water to a boil in a small saucepan over high heat, stirring constantly just until sugar dissolves. Then cook without stirring, occasionally swirling saucepan by handle to combine darker syrup at edges with clear syrup in center, until caramel is evenly golden brown, about 3 minutes. Pour an equal amount of caramel into 4 ramekins. Quickly tilt each ramekin to coat inside with caramel as well as you can. Repeat with remaining caramel and ramekins. (If caramel thickens, reheat until fluid again.)

Bring coconut milk to a simmer in a medium saucepan over high heat. Beat remaining ¾ cup sugar with eggs, yolks and vanilla in a medium bowl until eggs are pale yellow. Gradually whisk in hot coconut milk. Strain custard through a wire sieve into a large measuring cup. Pour equal amounts of custard into ramekins. Place ramekins in a large roasting pan.

Place roasting pan in oven, and pour hot water into pan to come halfway up sides of ramekins. Bake just until flans are set around edges (if you gently shake a ramekin, center will seem unset), about 25 minutes. Using tongs, remove ramekins from hot water and cool.

Cover each flan with plastic wrap and refrigerate until well chilled, at least 6 hours. (The flans can be made up to 2 days ahead, and then covered and refrigerated.)

To unmold, use your thumbs to gently press around diameter of each flan to release it from sides of its ramekin; do not cut around edges with a knife. Place ramekin upside down on a dessert plate. Holding ramekin and plate together, give them a firm shake to unmold flan. Lift off ramekin. Scrape any clinging caramel over flan. Repeat with remaining flans. Sprinkle each flan with toasted coconut. Serve chilled.

NOTE: To toast coconut, spread it on a rimmed baking sheet. Bake in a preheated 350°F oven, stirring occasionally, until golden brown, about 10 minutes. Cool completely.

CLOCKWISE FROM TOP LEFT:

Lilly with sisters Flo and Memsie, playing in the sand, 1930s.

Jumping grandkids, 2005.

Lilly with daughters Liza and Minnie, walking in the surf, 1960s.

"Mud Peeps," a.k.a. Emma Pulitzer and Rodman Leas, 1993.

Summer

"One summer the offspring of the Fowlers—of Mardi Gras fame—

came to Palm Beach en masse. They came and they came and

they came. I had seventeen people at every meal for two weeks.

How we survived without Martha I'll never know.

As the kids spent all their time in the jungle and since it was sooo hot,

we called it 'Camp Sweat in the Woods'. I loved it."

—LILLY

FOURTH OF JULY

"Waves waist high on the Fourth of July."

—PALM BEACH SURFERS' HOPE

*E*very July fourth, people from Juneau, Alaska, to Jupiter, Florida, celebrate the most all-American of holidays with parades, fairs, cookouts, picnics, concerts, fireworks displays and an outpouring of patriotism.

Palm Beach has a relatively low-key approach to Fourth of July celebrations, partly because the town began as a winter residence that literally closed down during summertime. There is a town fete and fireworks on Lake Worth, but nearly all the celebrations are family cookouts and picnics. It's one of the few days that Lilly cedes the party-giving reins to her daughter Minnie.

"Minnie and her husband Kevin have a really great beach picnic," says Lilly. "They take their tent, and lots of beach umbrellas, along with a couple of coolers, and set them up right by the ocean. The sun, the surf, the kids and the dogs—what could be better than that?"

Since food and drink is transported to the beach, the menu is kept deliciously simple. It includes good old-fashioned food like fried chicken, potato salad and tomato sandwiches, which are a special favorite of Lilly's. Everything is prepared in advance; nothing needs to be grilled or cooked that day.

"Growing up we spent a lot of our time at the beach—either at Piping Rock or we'd drive over to Jones Beach," Lilly says. "I was always black from the sun. Flo was beet red and one huge freckle. Memsie was under her hat and umbrella. What a trio! I still remember our picnics—with those soggy, sandy tomato sandwiches on white bread with mayo, salt and pepper and NO crusts."

Lilly has vivid memories of childhood Fourth of Julys spent in upstate New York. "We'd be on Long Island in the summer, but we'd always go up to Cooperstown to see our father, known by all of us as Pappy!

"I remember the black raspberry ice cream served in a sugar cone at the country club up in Cooperstown," Lilly says with a fond look in her eyes. "Pappy McKim had family there—our aunts, uncles and cousins. We also had a lot of family on our mother's side—our great uncle Ambrose Clarke and his wife Florence, who was my grandmother's sister. Uncle Brose owned most of Cooperstown and had the most beautiful

a beach picnic

TOMATO SANDWICHES WITH BASIL MAYONNAISE

SPICY DEVILED EGGS

CRUNCHY POTATO AND RADISH SALAD

MARINATED VEGETABLE SLAW

PERFECT OVEN-FRIED CHICKEN

BLUEBERRY-LEMON BARS

PLAIN WATERMELON WEDGES, PEELED ORANGES AND BUNCHES OF GRAPES

stable I've ever seen. Mother used to send our horses up and we'd ride every day. Uncle Brose would drive all over Cooperstown in his coach and four-in-hand (four beautifully matched horses). It was really an incredible sight. At the end of each drive, he would always stop at the houses of friends (who, in truth, he was most often related to; it was that kind of small town back then) and have a glass of pink champagne. He was a wonderful character."

Today Cooperstown is best known as the home of the Baseball Hall of Fame, but in the late 1930s and early 1940s, it was little more than a small village with a few extra families that would come up for the summer months.

"The Fourth of Julys were so special there," remembers Lilly. "There was a most wonderful parade from Springfield Center to Hyde Hall. It was totally all-American, with Boy Scouts and banners and flags. There were community sings.

"At the head of Otsego Lake, Tommy Goodyear had a sort of family compound with a huge boathouse, and they would have a picnic on Fourth of July night, just hot dogs and hamburgers. It was great fun. We'd play Spin the Bottle, or," Lilly continues with a laugh, "perhaps I should say Spin the Bottle was played. We had a crazy group: mostly our cousins, but a lot of the Busches (of the beer, not the presidents), too."

It might prove more difficult to spin the bottle on a sandy beach, but Lilly's group is still a little crazy. When they gather together on the beach, it's nothing but sheer fun and good times. It's a silly, casual day. There's swimming in the ocean, Frisbee games, tossing the ball with the dogs or just flopping on a cushion with the latest John Grisham and a tube of sunblock. People stay all day, or they drift in and out. Doesn't matter one bit.

"It's a beautiful day," says Lilly's son-in-law Kevin McCluskey. "Bright blue sky and gin-clear water. Everyone's in the water. The waves are great—waist high, breaking perfectly for adults and kids. I go out with my young son Jack sitting on the nose of my surfboard. It's fantastic."

As folks clamber out of the water, they're rewarded with some of Minnie's treats, like watermelon wedges, grapes and peeled oranges that have been stuffed into the refrigerator overnight so they are very, very cold. They are the perfect antidote to the hot sun and surf.

"We're on the beach for, oh my gosh, at least six hours," says Minnie. "And when the kids get tired from swimming, they make these elaborate sand castles, decorated with seashells and driftwood."

"Then at night," says Kevin, "we have this crazy extravaganza of fireworks way up on the north end of the island. We put on our own little show for a couple of hours."

"Or," laughs Minnie, "until the police find us and ask us to stop."

Best 4th of July celebration

Called "the greatest 4th on Earth," Boston's daylong party along the Charles River esplanade culminates with an outdoor concert by the Boston Pops. A rousing thirty-minute fireworks display accompanies Tchaikovsky's "1812 Overture," with cannons booming and local church bells pealing away. The esplanade is filled with picnickers and scores of small boats dot the Charles as families and friends celebrate on land and at sea.

From sea to shining sea

From New England to southern California there are unique opportunities to take an up-close look at different eras in America's history. July fourth is a most appropriate day to visit, for example, one of the presidential libraries and museums that honor our former chief executives.

Each library displays objects and memorabilia—from the retired Air Force One to the Emmy Award given to Dwight Eisenhower—pertaining to the presidencies of the men who governed through what will be known as "The American Century."

Herbert Hoover West Branch, IA
hoover.archives.gov

Franklin D. Roosevelt Hyde Park, NY
fdrlibrary.marist.edu

Harry S. Truman Independence, MO
trumanlibrary.org

Dwight D. Eisenhower Abilene, KS
eisenhower.archives.gov

John F. Kennedy Boston, MA
jfklibrary.org

Lyndon B. Johnson Austin, TX
lbjlib.utexas.edu

Richard M. Nixon Yorba Linda, CA
nixonfoundation.org

Gerald Ford Museum Ann Arbor, MI
fordlibrarymuseum.gov

Jimmy Carter Atlanta, GA
jimmycarterlibrary.gov

Ronald Reagan Simi Valley, CA
reaganlibrary.com

George H. W. Bush College Station, TX · bushlibrary.tamu.edu

William J. Clinton Little Rock, AK
clintonfoundation.org

Four 4th facts

The White House held its first Fourth of July reception in 1801. It had just opened the year before.

John Adams and Thomas Jefferson, the second and third U.S. presidents, both died on July 4, 1826, the fiftieth anniversary of the signing of the Declaration of Independence. Completing the hat trick, five years later, James Monroe, president number 5, also died on July 4.

On every Fourth of July, the Liberty Bell is gently tapped, not rung. No one wants its famous crack to expand!

Esther Friedman and Esther Pauline Friedman, also known as Dear Abby and Anne Landers, were born on July 4, 1918.

Tomato sandwiches with basil mayonnaise

These are only worth making with the best local tomatoes and really good bread. While Lilly's tomato sandwiches of long ago were made with plain mayonnaise, now that fresh basil is in every market, let's add the basil—and leave out the sand! 8 SANDWICHES

4 large ripe tomatoes, cored

Salt and freshly ground pepper, to taste

1 cup mayonnaise

⅓ cup finely chopped fresh basil

16 slices firm, sliced white sandwich bread, crusts trimmed

Slice tomatoes crosswise into ½-inch-thick rounds. Place tomatoes on paper towels and season with salt. Let stand for 30 minutes to exude juices. Pat off moisture with more paper towels. Season with pepper.

Mix mayonnaise and basil in a small bowl. Make 8 sandwiches, using 2 slices of bread, 2 tablespoons mayonnaise and half a tomato for each. Cut sandwiches as desired. Wrap tightly in waxed paper (preferred, so sandwiches can breathe) or plastic wrap. (The sandwiches can be made up to 8 hours ahead, and then wrapped and chilled in a refrigerator or ice chest. Remove from refrigerator or cooler 1 hour before serving.) Serve at room temperature.

Spicy deviled eggs

You can't have a picnic without deviled eggs. As befits their name, this filling is zestier than most versions. Using equal amounts of egg yolks and white halves will only give you a wimpy amount of filling, so plan on discarding some of the whites to beef up the proportion of yolks. A pastry bag does the best job of piping the filling, but a spoon works fine.

20 DEVILED EGG HALVES

1 dozen large eggs, hard-boiled (see Creamed Egg Gratin, page 34)

1/4 cup mayonnaise

2 tablespoons medium-hot chunky salsa, finely chopped

1/2 teaspoon chili powder

Salt and hot red pepper sauce, to taste

Strips of pickled jalapeño or red pepper or fresh parsley leaves, for garnish

Cut each egg in half lengthwise. Remove yolks. Discard 4 egg white halves or save for another use. Rub yolks through a wire sieve into a medium bowl. Stir in mayonnaise, salsa and chili powder. Season with salt and hot pepper sauce.

Fit a pastry bag with a large open star tip. Transfer yolk mixture to pastry bag. Pipe filling into whites. Garnish with jalapeño strips. Cover and refrigerate until ready to serve. (The eggs can be prepared up to 1 day ahead, and then covered and refrigerated. Transport to the picnic in a cooler.) Serve chilled.

Crunchy potato and radish salad

Some cooks seem to confuse potato salad with mashed potatoes, but no soggy, mushy potato salad here. This one is studded with crunchy bits like radishes and dill pickles. 8 TO 10 SERVINGS

3 pounds red potatoes, scrubbed but unpeeled

1/4 cup dill pickle juice

1/2 cup mayonnaise

1/2 cup sour cream

1 tablespoon Dijon mustard

1 cup sliced radishes (about 16 radishes)

1 cup (1/2-inch) diced dill pickle

6 scallions, white and green parts, thinly sliced

Salt and freshly ground pepper, to taste

2 tablespoons chopped fresh dill or parsley

Place whole potatoes in a large pot and add enough lightly salted water to cover. Cover with a lid and bring to a boil over high heat. Reduce heat to medium-low and simmer until potatoes are tender when pieced with a tip of a knife, about 25 minutes. Drain well. Cool until easy to handle, but still warm.

Cut potatoes into 1/2-inch-thick slices. Transfer warm potatoes to a large bowl. Sprinkle potatoes with dill pickle juice. Mix mayonnaise, sour cream and mustard in a small bowl. Pour over potatoes and mix gently. Add radishes, pickles and scallions, and mix again. Season with salt and pepper. Cover and refrigerate until well chilled, at least 2 hours. (The salad can be made 1 day ahead, and then covered and refrigerated. Transport to the picnic in a cooler.) Sprinkle with dill or parsley and serve chilled.

Marinated vegetable slaw

There are many different styles of cole slaw, and this one falls into the marinated category. The colorful mix of vegetables soaks up the sweet and sour dressing, making it a perfect candidate for preparing well ahead of the picnic. A food processor will slice and shred the vegetables in record time. 8 SERVINGS

1 head cabbage (2¼ pounds), cut into quarters and cored

1 red bell pepper, ribs and seeds removed

1 green bell pepper, ribs and seeds removed

4 large carrots

8 scallions, white and green parts, thinly sliced

⅓ cup distilled white vinegar

¼ cup sugar

1 tablespoon salt

½ teaspoon freshly ground pepper

⅓ cup vegetable oil

At least 4 hours before serving, fit a food processor with a slicing blade. Slice cabbage and transfer to a large bowl. Feed red and green peppers through feed tube to thinly slice them; add to bowl. Change to a shredding blade, and shred carrots. Transfer to bowl, and add scallions.

Whisk vinegar, sugar, salt and pepper in a medium bowl to dissolve sugar. Gradually whisk in oil. Pour over slaw and mix well. The slaw will seem dry at this point, but it will give off juices as it stands. Cover and refrigerate for at least 4 hours or overnight. (The slaw can be made up to 2 days ahead, and then covered and refrigerated. Transport to the picnic in a cooler.) Serve chilled, with a slotted spoon.

Perfect oven-fried chicken

Frying chicken in oil is a chore, but baking crumb-coated chicken is a pleasure. This is an easy recipe that makes a mountain of chicken in no time, once you allow two hours to marinate the chicken in buttermilk. 8 TO 10 SERVINGS

2 chickens, about 4 pounds each

2 cups buttermilk

1 tablespoon hot red pepper sauce

2 teaspoons salt

2½ cups Italian-flavored dried bread crumbs

1 teaspoon dried thyme

1 teaspoon dried basil

1 teaspoon dried oregano

1 teaspoon garlic powder

1 teaspoon freshly ground black pepper

8 tablespoons unsalted butter, melted

Cut each chicken into 2 drumsticks, 2 thighs, 2 wings and 2 breasts. Cut each breast half crosswise. You'll have 20 pieces total.

Mix buttermilk, hot sauce and salt in a large bowl. Add chicken pieces and mix to coat with buttermilk. Cover and refrigerate for at least 2 and up to 8 hours.

Position racks in upper and center of oven and preheat oven to 400°F. Line 2 large baking sheets with aluminum foil, and oil foil.

Mix bread crumbs, thyme, basil, oregano, garlic powder and pepper in a shallow dish. One piece at a time, remove chicken from bowl and shake off excess buttermilk. Roll in bread crumbs to coat and place on baking sheet. Drizzle chicken with melted butter.

Bake for 20 minutes. Switch positions of baking sheets from top to bottom and continue baking until chicken is golden brown and shows no sign of pink when pierced at thigh bone, about 20 minutes more. (The chicken can be made 8 hours ahead, and then covered and refrigerated. Transport to the picnic in a cooler. Remove 1 hour before serving.) Serve at room temperature.

Blueberry-lemon bars

You've had lemon bars before, but these will probably become your favorite version. The summery blueberries are a perfect match for the tangy lemon filling, and the almond-flavored crust pulls it all together. Try to use nonstick aluminum foil for lining the pan.

9 BARS

- ¾ cup all-purpose flour
- ½ cup sliced natural almonds
- ¼ cup confectioner's sugar, plus more for garnish
- 8 tablespoons (1 stick) unsalted butter, at room temperature, cut into thin slices
- ½ teaspoon almond extract
- 3 large eggs, at room temperature
- 1 cup granulated sugar
- Grated zest of 2 lemons
- ⅓ cup fresh lemon juice
- ¾ teaspoon baking powder
- ¼ teaspoon salt
- 1 cup fresh blueberries

Position rack in center of oven and preheat to 350ºF. Lightly butter an 8-inch-square baking pan. Fold a 14-inch piece of nonstick aluminum foil (or use regular aluminum foil) lengthwise to make an 8-inch-wide strip. Fit into pan, letting excess hang over sides to act as handles. If using regular foil, butter it well. Dust buttered areas of pan with flour and tap out excess flour.

Process flour, almonds and confectioner's sugar in a food processor fitted with a metal blade until almonds are ground to a powder. Add butter and pulse until dough begins to cling together. Sprinkle in almond extract and pulse a few more times. Press dough firmly and evenly into pan, letting it come about ¼ inch up sides. Bake until dough is set and lightly browned around edges, about 18 minutes.

Whisk eggs, sugar, lemon zest and juice, baking powder and salt in a medium bowl until well combined. Scatter blueberries in crust. Pour lemon mixture over berries. Return pan to oven and bake until filling is evenly risen and deep golden brown, about 25 minutes. Cool completely in pan on a wire cake rack.

Sift confectioner's sugar over filling. Run a sharp knife on two sides of pastry touching sides of pan to release it. Lift up on foil handles to remove pastry in one piece. Pull off and discard foil. Using a sharp knife dipped into hot water, cut pastry into 9 bars. (The bars can be stored in an airtight container, refrigerated, for up to 3 days. Transport to the picnic in a cooler.) Serve at room temperature.

BAD JACK'S SHARK ATTACK BIRTHDAY PARTY

"Why is he called Bad Jack McCluskey?
Because, he wasn't very good.
He was a true wild man."

—LILLY ON HER YOUNGEST GRANDSON

Though not up there with President's Day, Bastille Day or even Take Your Son or Daughter to Work Day, ask any kid if their birthday qualifies as a holiday and you'll get a resounding "YES" in response. And why not? It's a day when they, themselves, alone, are praised, sung to, given cake and ice cream and piled high with gifts.

Not to mention the party. A kid's birthday party is undoubtedly one of the highlights of their year. It can be big or small, lavish or simple. They don't care, really, because it will be a celebration honoring the day—five, ten, fifteen, sixteen years ago—when they were born. It's their day.

Now, Bad Jack—who, in reality, is a terrific little guy—is the youngest of Lilly's seven grandchildren. Growing up on an island—which, after all, is what Palm Beach is—has given him a natural fascination for all things aquatic. He swims, he fishes, he boats, he floats, he dives, he surfs, he sails. He's barely out of the water when he has a minute free. Coming home from school takes an hour because he has to stop at every bait store in town. Jack even has his own bait freezer at home (mom got tired of having her freezer stuffed with the day's catch).

Ask Jack his favorite fish of all and you get a fast response: shark. Shark? How'd that happen? Well, it's a combination of Jack's first dream where a shark played a prominent role, and the fried snapper at the Bath & Tennis Club that Jack mistook for shark, plus a trip to the Bahamas where the McCluskeys came across a school of nurse sharks while catching lobster. He's fascinated by sharks.

So when it comes time to celebrate Bad Jack's May 1st birthday, it's both fun and logical to use his favorite fish as the party's theme and make a Shark Attack Birthday Party.

It's not as hard as you'd think. Lilly is, after all, the Queen of the Shortcut. Grill up some fish ("Oh, you should know, any fish that Jack eats he labels 'shark,'" Lilly explains) grill up some hot dogs, serve some mac 'n' cheese and top it off with a shark-shaped cake.

Have the party near a place where Jack and his friends can fish and you're all set. A group of little boys happy as, well, clams. No party planners, no fuss and very little bother. The only two things you need to pull off a party like this are some thought and a little ingenuity.

a fishy birthday

GRILLED SHARK (OR ANY FISH) SANDWICHES WITH ORANGE MARINADE

GRILLED HOT DOGS

SHELLS AND CHEESE

SHARK CAKE

What makes a birthday party special is when it reflects who they are and what they like. A girl's passion for riding or the ballet, or a boy's for soccer or superheroes are easy starting points around which to build a party. Take a small group of their friends out to a baseball game, a Broadway show or a summer blockbuster movie followed by a pizza party and a cake.

Or stay at home. Amy Pulitzer, Lilly's daughter-in-law, says that when her daughter Emmy turned fifteen, "She wanted to have a Junior Spa Day, so that's what her party was. We had different beauty stations outside—facials, manicures, pedicures, cucumber eye masks—and all the girls rotated stations.

"We topped it off with a family tradition—the no-fail buttermilk birthday cake. It's heart-shaped and covered in whipped cream, strawberries and blueberries, and then topped with all those little plastic figures—you know, the toy soldiers and the dinosaurs. We have it every year for everyone in the family."

Whatever a kid likes to do best—be it riding or racing, playing with Tonka Toys or singing karaoke—it's easy to tailor a party to fit their interests. Just pull out one or two elements that you can easily manage—a game or activity, a special treat—and let the natural excitement of kids having a party take over.

"It was a hell of a lot easier in the old days," grouses Lilly good-naturedly. "We'd just throw them all into the pool, have a cake and call it a day."

"Oh, it was so much fun," remembers Minnie. "We'd be in the pool or up on the trampoline, and if we were up on the trampoline, they'd turn the hoses on us." Since Liza and Minnie have birthdays one day apart, their parties were sometimes combined. Minnie remembers birthday parties at a local roller rink where they would play fiendish rounds of Crack the Whip, and pity the poor soul who was on the end. It was not unknown to sustain a broken bone or two.

"It was all, 'Oh, let's have some fun,'" says Minnie.

"Yes," laughs Lilly, "and then go to the hospital."

Lilly remembers

"For special birthday parties when I was a girl, a group of us would be driven in to New York City. We'd have lunch and then go to a show—I remember seeing 'Oklahoma' and 'Annie Get Your Gun.' It was a true treat!"

Find your inner party

If the kids have seen JAWS one too many times (which may even be just once) and don't want to have a Shark Attack Birthday Party, well, of course the idea is to tailor the party to your child's interests and hobbies, whether that be football, foosball, ballet or bumper cars. Cater to your child's likes and you'll have a party filled with happy campers.

Top ten kids' party-planning tips

1. Let your kids in on the planning and preparation. It's the one time they're guaranteed to "jump to it" when it's time to do a task.

2. Rule of thumb: invite one guest for each year of your child's age. Keep it manageable.

3. Look to popular entertainment, movies, sports or TV in choosing a party theme.

4. Keep them busy with games and other activities.

5. Always have a plan B in case of bad weather, a flu epidemic or any unforeseen emergency.

6. Beware of sleepovers. With younger kids (10 and under), you're likely to lose half of them by midnight ("Mommy, I want to come home"). With older kids, they (and you) will get very little sleep.

7. And away we go! Amusement parks, recreation centers, swimming pools and ice skating rinks have all become popular locations for teenage parties.

8. Remember your party manners. "Thank-yous" are something one can never say (or write) too often. Thank-you notes that kids create—by hand or on the computer—are a fun way to start sharpening your young ones' social skills.

9. Make their day special. An alternative to a party might be a special celebration that becomes part of a unique birthday ritual. Try breakfast in bed, dinner in a favorite restaurant or a visit with Grandma.

10. Make memory books or scrapbooks with reminders of the day. Photographs, invitations, cards and so on can be added year after year. They will become a family treasure.

Still need help?

Try these online resources for inspiration:

amazingmoms.com

birthdayexpress.com

party411.com

kidsparties.com

creativekidsathome.com

partygamecentral.com

childparenting.about.com

Grilled shark (or any fish) sandwiches with orange marinade

Shark is Jack's favorite fish, so it's not hard to decide what the main course for his party will be—marinated grilled shark, tucked into rolls and served with tartar sauce. Shark has a distinctive meaty flavor and texture that is mellowed by this mildly acidic marinade.

12 SERVINGS

MARINADE

³/₄ **cup fresh orange juice**

¹/₃ **cup extra-virgin olive oil**

¹/₄ **cup red wine vinegar**

2 **teaspoons dried oregano**

3 **garlic cloves, chopped**

¹/₂ **teaspoon salt**

¹/₂ **teaspoon crushed hot red pepper flakes**

3 **pounds skinless shark steaks, cut into 4 or 5 manageable portions**

12 **soft sandwich rolls, toasted on grill**

1¹/₂ **cups Remoulade Sauce (page 17) or store-bought tartar sauce, for serving**

3 **cups shredded iceberg lettuce**

2 **large ripe tomatoes, thinly sliced**

To make marinade, shake orange juice, oil, vinegar, oregano, garlic, salt and hot pepper in a closed zippered plastic bag to combine. Add shark and marinate in refrigerator for 30 minutes to 1 hour, no longer.

Build a charcoal fire in an outdoor grill and let burn until coals are covered with white ash. For a gas grill, preheat on high. Lightly oil grill grate.

Remove shark from marinade. Place on grill and cover. Grill, turning once, until shark is opaque when flaked with tip of knife, 8 to 10 minutes. Transfer to a serving platter. Cut steak into pieces to fit rolls.

Make sandwiches with shark, rolls, Remoulade Sauce, lettuce and tomato slices. Serve hot.

Grilled hot dogs

12 hot dogs

12 hot dog buns, toasted on grill

Relish, mustard and ketchup, for serving

Build a charcoal fire in an outdoor grill and let burn until coals are covered with white ash. For a gas grill, preheat on high. Lightly oil grill grate.

Grill hot dogs, turning occasionally, until seared with grill marks and heated through, about 4 minutes. Serve hot, with the buns, relish, mustard and ketchup.

Shells and cheese

When it comes to macaroni 'n' cheese for kids, play it safe with mild cheeses. But, play up the nautical theme with shell-shaped pasta.

12 SERVINGS

1½ pounds shell-shaped pasta

10 tablespoons (1¼ sticks) unsalted butter, divided

½ cup plus 1 tablespoon all-purpose flour

1½ quarts milk, heated

3 cups (12 ounces) mild Cheddar cheese

2 cups (8 ounces) Monterey Jack cheese

Salt and freshly ground pepper, to taste

⅓ cup dried bread crumbs

⅓ cup freshly grated Parmesan cheese

Position rack in center of oven and preheat to 350°F. Lightly butter a 10 X 15-inch baking dish.

Bring a large pot of lightly salted water to a boil over high heat. Add pasta and cook until barely tender, about 8 minutes. Drain well. Return to pot.

Meanwhile, melt 9 tablespoons of butter in a large saucepan over medium-low heat. Whisk in flour. Let bubble without browning for 2 minutes. Whisk in milk and bring to a boil, whisking often, over high heat. Whisk in Cheddar and Jack cheeses. Season with salt and pepper.

Stir sauce into pasta in pot. Spread evenly in baking dish. Mix bread crumbs and Parmesan cheese and sprinkle over pasta. Dot remaining 1 tablespoon butter over crumbs. (The pasta can be prepared up to 8 hours ahead, and then cooled, covered and refrigerated.)

Bake until sauce is bubbling and top is golden brown, about 30 minutes (about 40 minutes if refrigerated). Let stand 5 minutes, then serve hot.

Shark cake

This cake is guaranteed to bring out the inner cake decorator in you. It's really very simple. Just follow the pattern for cutting out the pieces of baked cake and stick them together with frosting, and you'll end up with an adorable shark cake that everyone can sink their teeth into (Ha ha!). If you aren't up for it, your local bakery or supermarket is sure to be able to provide you with a nautically inspired cake.

12 SERVINGS

CAKE

6 ounces bittersweet chocolate, finely chopped

3 cups all-purpose flour

3 cups granulated sugar

12 tablespoons (1½ sticks) unsalted butter, thinly sliced, at room temperature

3 large eggs, at room temperature

1½ teaspoons baking soda

¾ teaspoon baking powder

¾ teaspoon salt

2¼ cups buttermilk, at room temperature

1½ teaspoons vanilla extract

CAKE FROSTING BASE

6 cups confectioner's sugar

12 tablespoons (1½ sticks) unsalted butter, at room temperature

2 teaspoons vanilla

½ cup milk, divided

Red or pink food coloring, for pink frosting

4 ounces unsweetened chocolate, finely chopped

Blue aluminum foil, for platter (see Note)

1 round red candy (such as Life Savers), for shark eye

Candy corn, for shark teeth

To make cake, position rack in center of oven and preheat to 350°F. Lightly butter a 15 X 10-inch glass baking pan. Line bottom with waxed paper. Dust sides of pan with flour and tap out excess.

Melt chocolate in top part of a double boiler over hot, not simmering, water. Remove from heat and cool until tepid.

Whisk flour, sugar, butter, eggs, baking soda, baking powder and salt in a large bowl. Add buttermilk and vanilla. Using an electric mixer on low speed (a heavy-duty standing mixer fitted with the paddle blade works best), mix for 30 seconds, scraping bowl often. Add chocolate. Increase speed to high, and mix, scraping often, for 3 minutes to make a very smooth batter. Spread batter evenly in pan.

Place pan in oven and immediately reduce oven temperature to 325°F. Bake until a wooden toothpick inserted in center of cake comes out clean, about 35 minutes. Transfer to a wire cake rack and cool for 10 minutes. Run a knife around inside of pan to release cake. Invert onto chopping board and then remove pan and waxed paper. Place large cake rack on top and invert cake right side up. Remove board and cool completely.

To make frosting base, sift confectioner's sugar into a medium bowl. Add butter and vanilla. Beat with electric mixer on medium speed, adding about ⅓ cup milk to bring frosting to thick, spreading consistency.

To make white frosting (for shark belly), mix 1¼ cups frosting base with 3 tablespoons milk in a small bowl. For pink frosting (for inside of mouth), mix ¼ cup frosting base with a few drops red or pink food coloring. For chocolate frosting (for shark body), melt chocolate in top part of double boiler over hot, not simmering, water. Remove from heat and cool until tepid. Mix remaining frosting with melted chocolate and 3 tablespoons water.

Using a serrated knife, cut shark body, fins and tail from chocolate cake (see pattern). If you don't have an appropriate platter, line a large cake board, platter or baking sheet with aqua or blue cake foil. Place shark body on platter. Slip strips of waxed paper under cake to protect foil.

Using a large metal icing spatula, frost shark belly area with white frosting. Refrigerate or set in cool place to set icing. Frost shark body (leave inside of mouth unfrosted), fin and tail with chocolate frosting. Attach fin and tail to body with additional chocolate frosting. Place round candy on body for shark eye. Using small metal icing spatula, frost inside of mouth with pink frosting. Insert candy teeth, pointed sides out, into mouth area for shark teeth. Refrigerate to set icing. (Cake can be prepared 1 day ahead, and then covered loosely with plastic wrap and stored at room temperature.) Discard waxed paper. Cut into slices to serve.

NOTE: Blue cake foil is available at cake-decorating supply shops and by mail order from thebakerskitchen.com.

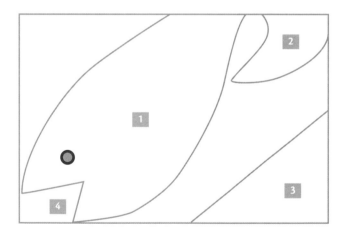

1. Shark body.
2. Reverse and trim for tail.
3. Trim for top fin.
4. Trim for second tail fin.

(Enlarge pattern approximately 450%, if needed.)

LABOR DAY
WEEKEND

*"It's my mission in life to keep
you freeloaders fed!"*

—LILLY, ON HOUSEGUESTS IN GENERAL

The only peeps I have ever asked to stay are my closest amigos from the class of '49," says Lilly, referring to her Farmington pals. "As for everybody else, they just show up. I've had people come for a week and stay for three months."

Once you've had the experience of being Lilly's houseguest, it's difficult to imagine how anyone could bear to leave after only ninety days. As you walk through her turquoise front door, an instantaneous refrain—"Forget your troubles. C'mon, get happy."—enters your subconscious, and you just feel good.

Casa Lilly is big, and yet it manages to be cozy at the same time so that the atmosphere is welcoming. One room opens onto another in a relaxed way, inviting you in rather than saying, "Ain't I grand." It's no wonder that the house is continually filled.

"It's very nice to be here by myself," Lilly says. "It feels like a one-bedroom house when I'm alone, not that I often get the chance. We used to have these wonderful Cuban weekends for Labor Day. Friends of Enrique's would come up from Pompano and Miami; we'd have four or five couples staying with us, and then, of course, the rest of the town would come over. They were the best. So much spirit. So much life."

Lilly remembers those days as "dancing, swimming and lots of gin rummy. They played hard, they were out for blood. There were teams and they would battle for hours, with the cigars and the laughing and screaming. The birdcage was next to the table and the poor birds were always croaking—from the cigars and the incredible expressions.

"Enrique loved to go out on our boat, so every Sunday out we'd go. The boat only held eight, but never left our dock without fifteen or twenty. It looked like the Bay of Pigs invasion. Miguel, our dear friend, was the 'steward' on the *Lilly II*. We'd drop anchor, swim, drink, turn on the radio. Bloody Marys started flowing at 10:00 and kept on until we hit the dock again (promptly by 1:30 for lunch). WA—HOO!"

a weekend menu

ARRIVAL EVENING SUPPER

SHRIMP GAZPACHO

LABOR DAY BARBECUE

BARBECUED BABY RIBS WITH GUAVA GLAZE

CHOPPED FARMSTAND SALAD

FLO'S CORN PUDDING

BARBECUED BAKED BEANS

SUMMER BERRY COBBLER WITH CINNAMON BISCUIT TOPPING

DEPARTURE DAY BRUNCH

SAUSAGE AND SUMMER VEGETABLE FRITTATA

PEACH MUFFINS WITH PECAN STREUSEL

LEFT: Friends arrive at Lilly's front door. RIGHT: Lilly (left) and friends frolic off the *Lilly II*, 1976.

Weekend life was centered around the pool, so bathing suits were the uniform of the day. Pareos, T-shirts, anything loose and comfortable were added as needed. At night, women would don caftans and everyone would congregate in Lilly's big living room. "We would never stop singing," Lilly says. "I had two pianos in the living room, so four hands on each piano. We had friends who played the guitar and sang, and an incredible doctor who played the bongo. The casa really rocked. The Cubans brought true fun and flavor to Palm Beach. How nice was that?"

From Palm Beach to Bucks County to the Berkshires and beyond, weekend getaways are a great way to gather a group of friends together to celebrate anything from a major holiday to simply the camaraderie they share. Remember, as Lilly says, you don't have to have a reason to have a party. "We'd make one up, so when hula hoops came out, we had a party."

But Labor Day offers a four-day weekend, as well as those bittersweet last days of summer that are especially nice to share with old friends. The corn is perfect. It's the last of the really great tomatoes. Blueberries are at their peak.

It's the one last chance for a great barbeque, which could be the centerpiece meal of the weekend. Everyone can chip in and help, from preparing to cooking and setting the table. Everyone, no matter what age, gets a task so they all feel part of the gang. As Lilly often says, when it comes to cooking, "I take every shortcut in the Western world." Nothing wrong with that. If you're in a Martha-Mode, you can whip up something special. Nothing wrong with that either.

Does Lilly have anything special that she does to prepare for her never-ending stream of houseguests? Does she place fresh flowers in an attractive vase on a table by the bed? Does she make sure there is a delicious selection of candies and biscuits waiting on the bureau? Does she buy an array of the latest fashion magazines?

"I make sure there are three rolls of toilet paper and a clean bar of soap in each bathroom, and that's it," she laughs.

Well, OK, that's the host's responsibility. How about the guests? What makes for a perfect house-guest (or, at least, one who hopes to be invited back)? With old friends, it's easier, for there's a cozy familiarity and a shared history of who's grumpy in the morning and who tends to cheat at Scrabble.

For the newbie, the best advice is to be aware. Sense when it's time to join in—in a mealtime conversation or an afternoon game of tennis—and sense when it's time to entertain yourself—when the house quiets down is always a good time to tuck in with a book or watch a movie.

Whatever you do, don't follow Lilly's lead—at least in this one specific example of houseguest etiquette. "I was staying with friends in St. Louis. This was back in my heavy smoking days. They had a wonderful dinner party for me and how did I repay them? I left a cigarette smoldering right in the middle of their gigantic white sofa. Can you imagine!!! I was the kind of houseguest one does not want in their house."

After a performance like that, what can one do about a hostess gift? "I sent a ton of caviar, but somehow I don't think that helped," Lilly says. In general, how does one go about choosing those tangible little "thank yous" that would make your mummy proud. The cardinal rule for choosing little "thank yous"—and this may come as a shock—is no candles and no scented soap. "They're cop-out gifts. Please, put a little thought into it," asserts the noted Palm Beach hostess with disdain.

Think about where your hosts' interests lie, and let that be your guide. As she spends so much time in her kitchen, Lilly says, "I'm always asking for pot holders, and no one ever gets them for me." Gardeners might appreciate a huge sack of tulip bulbs. Oenophiles would welcome a lovely pair of wine coasters. A lavishly illustrated coffee-table book never fails, especially if its subject—be it the saga of the victorious Boston Red Sox or Andrew Moore's photographs of Cuba in glorious decline—is close to your hosts' heart.

If all else fails, the ubiquitous pot of jam always works. There are many choices beyond the standard raspberry and strawberry. Lilly's pantry is stocked with a variety of mouthwatering treats like Italian tomato jam, red and green pepper jelly, mayhaw and guava jellies and calamondin marmalade.

Whatever you do, don't go overboard. A hostess gift is a gesture to indicate courtesy, not to overawe with grandiosity. "People care what other people think about them too much," says Lilly.

And her rules for being a good houseguest?

"Pick up your cans, water bottles and towels, or else I get very grumpy."

"IF you are still smoking (ugh), empty your ashtray."

"Don't unload the dishwashers. I go nuts when stuff is put in the wrong place (an aging thing)."

"Agree with everything I say—sure!!"

Anything else? "Yes, always remember," Lilly says with a grin, "it's Labor Day, so put your white shoes away."

The well-stocked beverage center

"So few people drink, haven't you noticed," says Lilly. "In the old days I was always ordering booze and keeping the cigarette boxes filled. No more. But I suppose you should always have:

Some wine, red and white

Clamato juice

Beef broth for Bloody Bulls

I always have vodka around

Rums, light and dark

One person you know always drinks Bourbon

Very few drink gin nowadays, but you have to have some

A good scotch

Cranberry, tangerine, grapefruit and orange juices

Diet Coke®, Classic Coke®, Sprite® and ginger ale

Tequila

Triple Sec

Beer

Tonic and soda water

Limes and lemons

Worcestershire and Tabasco sauce

Great getaways

"In the old days," Lilly recalls, "Labor Day used to be when people closed their houses down for the season and came back into the city." If you're saddled with those sorts of genteel friends, here are some delightful destinations where you can get the same joys of a country weekend visit without having to bring a gift or write a thank-you note afterward.

Cooperstown, New York In order to fully savor this upstate New York paradise, avoid the Baseball Hall of Fame Weekend. The Cooper Inn and Otesaga Resort Hotel are both luxury hotels, while the Blue Mingo Inn offers a charming B&B alternative.

Newport, Rhode Island This thriving seaport town offers two centuries worth of splendid American architectural history. Vanderbilt Hall Hotel, in the center of town, and the Chanler Hotel, at the start of the Cliff Walk, are two small but delightful hotels in the midst of the Gilded Age "cottages."

Camden, Maine The rugged coast of Maine has long drawn the hardiest of outdoor lovers to its summer pleasures. Norumbega, an elegant small hotel, is a stone manor house overlooking Penobscot Bay. It is close to sailing, golf, tennis and hiking.

Mackinac Island, Michigan Picture yourself in white linen, strolling out on the lawn for a game of croquet—that's the image that the Grand Hotel immediately brings to mind. This American classic dating from the Victorian era today offers golf, tennis, swimming, cycling, riding, special children's programs and horse drawn carriage tours, as well as croquet.

Jackson Hole, Wyoming The Amangani Resort, with its spectacular mountain views, is among the most magnificent retreats in the world. Personally guided fishing expeditions and hiking trips are but two of the varied activities offered. With a ratio of two staff to each guest, you feel as if you're staying with close friends in their luxurious country home.

Five books for every guest room:

1. a good biography

2. the new John Grisham

3. a short, funny novel (anyone from Evelyn Waugh to David Sedaris)

4. any Dominick Dunne

5. *Valley of the Dolls* (for your friends' trashy reading pleasure)

Shrimp gazpacho

Gazpacho is a way to savor ripe tomatoes and it doesn't require you to turn on the stove. It is also perfect for serving on the Friday night of a holiday weekend when you don't know exactly when guests will arrive. Just stand the bowl of gazpacho in a larger bowl of ice, and let guests help themselves, adding toppings as they like.

8 TO 10 SERVINGS

5 large ripe beefsteak tomatoes (about 2½ pounds)

5 medium Kirby cucumbers, scrubbed but unpeeled, and coarsely chopped

1 yellow bell pepper, seeded and coarsely chopped

2 garlic cloves, crushed through a press

3 cups tomato-vegetable juice, such as V-8

Salt and freshly ground black pepper, to taste

TOPPINGS

¾ pound cooked baby shrimp

Croutons, chopped tomatoes, chopped cucumbers, chopped yellow or red bell pepper and sliced scallions

Cut each tomato in half crosswise. Use fingers to push out seeds. Cut tomatoes into 2-inch chunks.

In batches, pulse tomatoes, cucumbers, bell pepper and garlic in a food processor fitted with a metal blade until coarsely chopped. Do not purée. Transfer to a large bowl and stir in juice. Cover and refrigerate until well chilled, at least 2 hours.

Just before serving, season gazpacho with salt and pepper. Place baby shrimp, croutons, tomatoes, cucumbers, bell pepper and scallions in individual bowls. Serve gazpacho chilled, topping each serving with a big spoonful of shrimp. Allow each guest to add other ingredients to taste.

Barbecued baby ribs with guava glaze

Lilly loves Caribbean flavors, and these succulent ribs go Latin with a bold spice rub and a tropical guava glaze. To ensure moist and tender ribs, the slabs are wrapped in aluminum foil and cooked on the grill in their own juices. Removed from the foil, they are then grilled again to brown them up and finished with a slathering of the sweet-tart glaze.

8 TO 10 SERVINGS

1 tablespoon salt

1 tablespoon dried thyme

1½ teaspoons ground allspice

1½ teaspoons ground ginger

1 teaspoon freshly ground black pepper

½ teaspoon cayenne pepper

8 pounds baby back ribs, cut into slabs of 10 ribs each

GUAVA GLAZE

2 tablespoons vegetable oil

1 medium onion, finely chopped

2 garlic cloves, minced

One 16-ounce jar guava jelly

2 tablespoons spicy brown or Dijon mustard

2 tablespoons red wine vinegar

2 tablespoons soy sauce

Mix salt, thyme, allspice, ginger, black pepper and cayenne in a small bowl. Rub mixture all over ribs. Wrap each slab tightly in a double thickness of aluminum foil. Set aside while building the fire.

Build a charcoal fire in an outdoor grill and let burn until coals are covered with white ash. For a gas grill, preheat on high, then adjust to medium.

Place foil-wrapped ribs on the grill and cover. Cook, turning occasionally, until ribs are tender (open foil to check), about 45 minutes. (The ribs can be prepared 2 hours ahead, and kept at room temperature. To store longer, cool and refrigerate for up to 8 hours.)

Meanwhile, make glaze. Heat oil in a medium saucepan over medium heat. Add onion and cook, stirring often, until golden, about 5 minutes. Add garlic and cook until fragrant, about 1 minute. Stir in guava jelly, mustard, vinegar and soy sauce and bring to a boil. Transfer to a medium bowl set in a larger bowl of iced water to cool and thicken.

Add more charcoal to the fire and let burn until medium-hot. You should be able to hold your hand at grill level for about 3 seconds. For a gas grill, maintain heat at medium.

Lightly oil the grill. Unwrap ribs and and place on grill. Slather tops of ribs with glaze. Cover and grill until undersides are browned, about 5 minutes. Turn, brush tops with glaze, cover and grill until undersides are glazed, about 2 minutes. Turn and grill to glaze other sides, about 2 minutes. Transfer ribs to cutting board and let stand 5 minutes. Cut between bones into individual ribs. Serve hot.

Chopped farmstand salad

Creativity is the keynote of this salad. A trip to a farm-stand or farmer's market will reveal what is in season, but at Labor Day, it's likely to be tomatoes, corn, summer squash and lettuce. Just use this recipe as inspiration, and buy whatever looks and tastes good.

8 TO 10 SERVINGS

1 medium head romaine lettuce (13 ounces), chopped into ½-inch pieces

3 large ripe tomatoes, preferably a combination of different colors and varieties, seeded and cut into ½-inch dice

1½ cups fresh corn kernels (cut from about 3 ears)

1 medium zucchini, cut into ¼-inch dice

1 medium yellow squash, cut into ¼-inch dice

2 celery ribs, cut into ¼-inch dice

½ cup thinly sliced radishes

1 garlic clove, crushed

½ cup packed basil leaves

3 tablespoons red wine vinegar

1 cup extra-virgin olive oil

Salt and freshly ground pepper, to taste

Mix lettuce, tomatoes, corn, zucchini, yellow squash, celery and radishes in a large bowl.

With the machine running, drop garlic through the feed tube of a food processor fitted with a metal blade or blender. Add basil and pulse until finely chopped. With machine running, add vinegar, then oil. Season with salt and pepper.

Pour over vegetables and toss well. Season again with salt and pepper and serve.

Flo's corn pudding

Lilly's sister Flo is downright famous for this melt-in-your-mouth pudding. Her recipe states "FRESH, not frozen or canned, corn kernels," and when you taste it, you won't want to do it any other way. 8 SERVINGS

2 tablespoons unsalted butter, softened, for the dish

2 cups fresh corn kernels (cut from about 6 ears cooked corn)

2 cups heavy cream

4 large eggs

2 tablespoons all-purpose flour

1 teaspoons salt

¼ teaspoon freshly ground pepper

2 tablespoons freshly grated Parmesan cheese

Position rack in center of oven and preheat oven to 375°F. Heavily butter a round 1½- to 2-quart baking dish or soufflé mold.

Purée corn in a food processor fitted with a steel chopping blade; scrape into a large bowl. Add heavy cream, eggs, flour, salt, and pepper, and whisk until smooth. Pour into baking dish and sprinkle cheese on top. Place baking dish in a larger roasting pan and pour hot water into pan to come ½-inch up side of baking dish.

Bake until pudding is puffed and a knife inserted in center comes out almost clean, about 1 hour. Let stand 5 minutes, then serve hot.

Barbecued baked beans

What's a barbecue without a big pot of baked beans in a thick cloak of sweet and tangy sauce? If you wish, the beans can be cooked on a covered grill, not directly over the coals or heat source, for about 1 hour.

8 TO 10 SERVINGS

5 bacon slices

1 tablespoon vegetable oil

2 medium onions, chopped

One 12-ounce can carbonated cola beverage

1 cup tomato ketchup

$\frac{1}{3}$ cup unsulfured "light" molasses

$\frac{1}{4}$ cup spicy brown mustard

1 tablespoon Worcestershire sauce

Two 15- to 19-ounce cans Great Northern beans, drained and rinsed

Two 15- to 19-ounce cans pink beans, drained and rinsed

Position rack in center of oven and preheat oven to 350ºF. Cook bacon in a Dutch oven over medium heat until crisp and browned, about 6 minutes. Transfer to paper towels to drain, leaving fat in pot; coarsely chop bacon.

Add vegetable oil to pot and heat. Add onions and cook, stirring often, until golden, about 6 minutes. Add cola, ketchup, molasses, mustard and Worcestershire sauce, and bring to a boil. Stir in beans and reserved bacon.

Cover and bake for 45 minutes. Uncover and bake until liquid is thick and syrupy, about 15 minutes more. Serve hot.

Summer berry cobbler with cinnamon biscuit topping

Bring out the vanilla ice cream to serve with this warm cobbler, bursting with summery flavor. Any combination of berries will do. Brown sugar not only sweetens the berries, but intensifies their color. 8 SERVINGS

FILLING

2 pints fresh strawberries, hulled and cut into halves

$1\frac{1}{2}$ pints fresh blueberries

$1\frac{1}{2}$ pints fresh raspberries

$1\frac{1}{2}$ pints fresh blackberries

$\frac{3}{4}$ cup packed light brown sugar

2 tablespoons cornstarch

3 tablespoons unsalted butter, thinly sliced

CINNAMON BISCUIT TOPPING

2 cups all-purpose flour

$\frac{1}{3}$ cup granulated sugar

2 teaspoons baking powder

1 teaspoon ground cinnamon

$\frac{1}{4}$ teaspoon salt

8 tablespoons (1 stick) unsalted butter, chilled, thinly sliced

$\frac{1}{2}$ cup half-and-half

1 large egg

1 teaspoon vanilla extract

Vanilla ice cream, for serving

Position rack in center of oven and preheat oven to 400°F. Lightly butter a deep, round 3-quart glass or ceramic baking dish.

To make filling, mix strawberries, blueberries, raspberries, blackberries, brown sugar and cornstarch in a medium bowl. Spread in a baking dish. Top with butter slices.

To make topping, whisk flour, sugar, baking powder, cinnamon and salt in a medium bowl. Add butter and use a pastry blender or two forks to cut butter into flour until mixture resembles coarse meal with a few pea-size pieces of butter. Mix half-and-half, egg and vanilla in a measuring cup. Stir liquid into flour mixture and mix just until combined. Using a tablespoon, drop 8 mounds of dough over fruit.

Bake for 20 minutes. Tent dish loosely with foil. Continue baking until berry juices are bubbling throughout and biscuits are golden brown and cooked through, about 20 minutes more. Serve hot or warm, with ice cream.

Sausage and summer vegetable frittata

The beauty of a frittata is its equally good hot from the oven or cooled off a bit to room temperature. To shorten the prep time in the morning, sauté the sausage and vegetables the night before, and simply warm them up in the skillet before completing the frittata. 8 SERVINGS

8 ounces sweet Italian sausage, casings removed

3 tablespoons extra-virgin olive oil, divided

1 large zucchini, trimmed, halved lengthwise and cut into ¼-inch slices

1 small red bell pepper, seeded and cut into ¼-inch dice

8 large eggs

¾ teaspoon salt

¼ teaspoon hot red pepper sauce

½ cup shredded smoked mozzarella

Chopped fresh basil, for serving

Position rack in center of oven and preheat to 350°F. Cook sausage in a 10-inch nonstick skillet over medium heat, breaking up with a spoon, until sausage shows no sign of pink, about 10 minutes. Transfer to a bowl with a slotted spoon; discard fat in skillet.

Heat 1 tablespoon of oil in skillet over medium heat. Add zucchini and red pepper and cook, stirring occasionally, until zucchini is barely tender, about 10 minutes. Transfer to bowl with sausage. (The sausage and vegetables can be prepared the night before making the frittata, and then cooled, covered and refrigerated. Heat them together in a skillet over medium heat, then transfer to a bowl before proceeding.)

Heat remaining 2 tablespoons oil in skillet over medium-low heat. Whisk eggs, salt and hot pepper sauce in a medium bowl until combined. Add sausage and vegetables. Pour egg mixture into skillet and cook until edges begin to set. Using a rubber spatula, lift up edge of frittata, and tilt skillet so uncooked eggs run underneath frittata. Continue cooking, occasionally lifting frittata and tilting skillet as described, until eggs are almost set, 4 to 5 minutes. Sprinkle with mozzarella. Bake until top is puffed and lightly browned, about 5 minutes.

Place a plate over top of skillet and invert frittata onto plate. Cut into wedges and sprinkle with basil. Serve hot or cooled to room temperature.

Peach muffins with pecan streusel

When houseguests smell the aroma of these peach-topped muffins wafting through the house, they won't stay in bed for long. To speed mixing the batter in the morning, prepare the dry ingredients and make the streusel the night before. To peel the peaches, drop them into boiling water for a minute or so, just to loosen the skins. Drain, rinse the peaches under cold water and then use a small knife to remove the skins.

1 DOZEN

2½ cups all-purpose flour

1 teaspoon baking powder

1 teaspoon baking soda

½ teaspoon salt

8 tablespoons (1 stick) unsalted butter, at room temperature

1 cup granulated sugar

2 large eggs, at room temperature

1 teaspoon vanilla extract

1 cup sour cream, at room temperature

3 ripe peaches, peeled, pitted and each cut into 8 wedges

PECAN STREUSEL

¼ cup packed light brown sugar

2 tablespoons unsalted butter, at room temperature

2 tablespoons all-purpose flour

½ teaspoon ground cinnamon

¼ cup finely chopped pecans

Position rack in center of oven and preheat oven to 350°F. Lightly butter 12 nonstick muffin cups. (Do not use plain muffin tins, or streusel may stick to top of pan.)

Sift flour, baking powder, baking soda and salt together. Beat butter and sugar in a medium bowl with an electric mixer on high speed until mixture is light and fluffy, about 3 minutes. One at a time, beat in eggs, then vanilla. On low speed, beat in three additions of flour, alternating with two additions of sour cream, and mix just until combined.

Divide batter equally among muffin cups. Top each muffin with 2 peach wedges.

For the streusel, rub brown sugar, butter, flour and cinnamon in a small bowl with fingers to combine. Work in pecans. Lightly pat streusel over tops of muffins.

Bake until muffins are golden brown and a wooden toothpick inserted in center of muffin comes out clean, 20 to 25 minutes. Cool in pans for 5 minutes. Carefully lift muffins to remove from tins. Serve warm or cooled to room temperature.

CLOCKWISE FROM TOP LEFT:

Lilly with sisters Flo and Memsie, 1940s.

General Honey's birthday party *(see page 128)*, 1964.

Lilly circa 1968.

Lilly's mother and stepfather, Mr. and Mrs. Ogden Phipps, Misses Flossie, Memsie and Lilly McKim, and their cousin Miss Electra Bostwick, 1949.

Fall

"Growing up, fall meant only one thing to me: hunt season.

We all loved to hunt, so every weekend we would head for the country on

Friday afternoon. Saturday we got up at 5:00. Memsie always rode sidesaddle,

looking incredible with Flo and I hanging on for dear life.

Our groom Johnny always rode with us—I guess to pick us up if we were

thrown. Over the years the three of us must have galloped through every

field and jumped over every fence and chicken coop in Long Island."

—LILLY

HALLOWEEN

"It's the night when you haven't a clue
who'll be there—little ghosties, big goblins
or something the cat dragged in."

—JERRY BEEBE, A FRIFND OF LILLY'S

Worth Avenue, the Palm Beach home of Van Cleef & Arpels, Hermés and Chanel, has long been accustomed to opening its doors to the wealthy, the glamorous, the chic. Yet one day each year, these retailers de luxe welcome a phalanx of miniature ghouls, goblins and SpongeBobs, each eager to sample their wares.

Diamonds, scarves and slingback pumps? Nope.

Think candy corn, chocolate bars and gummy bears, for it's the annual Worth Avenue Halloween Party. Kids in costumes scamper up and down the street, going from one store to the next, filling up their trick-or-treat bags with cheerful abandon.

The afternoon's high point is definitely the costume contest held in the Gucci courtyard. The stage is packed with dozens of kids competing for the highly coveted trophy for best costume. This being Palm Beach, some of the costumes are extravagant, others elaborate and a few completely over the top.

The year Bad Jack McCluskey won, he went as an astronaut wearing a costume his mother found for $8.99 in a local store! In addition to his trophy, his parents won a weekend at the swanky Brazilian Court hotel. "He got up on that stage," laughs his mother, Minnie, "and he just became this astronaut. If you could have seen the look on his face. It was so determined, so serious. It was hysterical."

"The key to all this stuff," adds father Kevin, "is that he truly believes in a make-believe world. This year he was a pirate and he learned all the words to Jimmy Buffett's song 'A Pirate Looks at 40.' He sang it all the time."

"Jack just has this true belief in make-believe and adventure," adds his doting Grannie. "How great is that?"

Apart from the Worth Avenue festivities, Halloween in Palm Beach is similar to that in towns across the country. Families congregate around their streets and walk up and down, going from house to house. Lilly's first house on the island was on Seaview and she would take her three kids up and down the streets, "sometimes dressed as either a pumpkin or a witch, depending on my mood," says she. That area was, is and will

A halloween party

HOT CRANBERRY-APPLE PUNCH

TWO-SALMON SPREAD WITH FRESH VEGETABLES

SWEET AND SPICY MEATBALLS

EL GRANDE CUBAN SANDWICH

ROASTED PUMPKIN SALSA WITH TORTILLA CHIPS

HALLOWEEN SUGAR COOKIES

always be kiddy delight; the families go all out and turn their backyards into a Booga-Booga Spookyville. Cobwebs, graveyards, eerie music, skeletons, ghosts—all the usual ghouly stuff—are there to get you in the mood.

Lilly's kids have fond memories of Halloweens past. "I used to have this wagon," remembers her son Peter. "It was one of those low ones that you'd pull around, and I'd lug it behind me on Halloween and just fill it up with candy." A generation later, the same tradition—and the same route—still held fast, but with one little difference. "When it was my turn to take my kids trick-or-treating, all of the parents would sit in the back of my friend Nellie's truck," recounts Liza, "and we'd drive up and down the streets trailing the kids while Bobby and Chris ran from door to door."

Liza's two boys are now young men, and that's a good thing, as over the years Halloween has come to rival New Year's Eve as the most popular party night of the year, especially so with the young 20s set. That post-college crowd, though far too sophisticated for a "kegger" party, still enjoys the chance to let loose. Halloween, and the opportunity it brings to don costumes and masks, adds an element of mystery and excitement to the evening. And perhaps even a hint of romance?

For Lilly, donning a costume and having fun has never been limited to just one night a year. From her early childhood days dressing up as a little Dutch maid for dinner to the lively theme parties she gave for Enrique's birthdays, Lilly seems to have worn a costume on just about every day but October thirty-first.

"I remember a great costume party that Mother and Ogden had for all of us," says Lilly. "They came as Mrs. McGregor and Farmer and my sisters and I were Flopsy, Mopsy and Cottontail. Our cousin Electra was Peter Rabbit and my brother Dinny was an adorable little clown. I know it wasn't Halloween; it was summer on Long Island. They had this incredible printed tent, with lace curtains. Lester Lanin's orchestra played, and the bunnies went wild!

"Memsie, Flo and I were very sophisticated bunnies. Our suits were white plush. We had high-heeled pink satin pumps with pink fishnet stockings, fat bunny tails and big perky ears! We never stopped laughing. Everything was so much fun. It was crazy."

Smarty party

Halloween is an opportune time to combine two worthwhile elements: helping out a good cause and having a great party. As an example, Lilly is known among her friends to be an animal lover. She is especially protective of the wild cats that live in Palm Beach; several of them call her jungle home. One recent Halloween she lent her support to a Scardy Cat Bash.

"It was quite a rumble that Halloween party for our island's feral cats' Palm Beach Cat Rescue," Lilly says. "The room was wonderfully sinister, the DJ spun some spooky tunes and we all danced and pranced, taking turns to squeeze and jig around with baby Jack (he was very good then; he hadn't become Bad Jack yet). Jack was dressed as one really fat little pumpkin. We raised a good bit of money, had a blast and helped the cats. Not too shabby, tabby!"

The great parties at Lilly's so often involved costumes and themes, so why not throw a themed Halloween costume party? Have people come as their favorite:

Vamp

Character from fiction

Person in history

Cartoon character

Villain

Hero

Movie star

Scary movie

You're back from trick-or-treating. The Halloween party's over. It's late, it's dark, it's quiet. It's the PERFECT time to pop up some corn and pop in a scary DVD. Here's a list of our faves:

Friday the 13th, Part 2 The best of them all, as it stars Lilly's daughter-in-law Amy as the heroine Ginny Field.

The Ring If you watch the tape, you only have seven days to live. Better to stick to the DVD…

Rosemary's Baby Did the devil make her do it? Mia Farrow shines in this masterpiece by Roman Polanski.

Scream 1, 2 and 3 It's a rare movie series that can scare you while making you laugh at the same time. Here's a hat trick, involving the creepy saga of Sidney Prescott, Gale Weathers and Deputy Dewey.

The Exorcist We know the devil made her do it. The DVD comes with footage deemed too outrageous for the 70s. Hard to imagine!

Hot cranberry-apple punch

For Halloween, how about this warm cranberry-apple drink, redolent with cinnamon and other spices? Small lady apples make an attractive garnish. Place a bottle of dark rum alongside the punch so each guest can spike it up (or not). 16 SERVINGS

Four (3-inch) cinnamon sticks

4 star anise (available at Asian grocers and many supermarkets)

2 teaspoons whole allspice

1 teaspoon whole cloves

1½ quarts apple juice

1½ quarts cranberry juice

1 dozen lady apples, for garnish

Dark rum, for serving

Rinse and squeeze dry a piece of cheesecloth. Wrap cinnamon, star anise, allspice and cloves in cheesecloth and tie into a packet with kitchen string.

Bring apple juice, cranberry juice and spices to a simmer in a large nonreactive saucepan over medium heat. Add apples. Transfer pot to a warming plate to keep warm. (Or reduce heat under pot to very low and serve punch from kitchen.)

Serve hot, with the rum on the side.

Two-salmon spread with fresh vegetables

3 CUPS, ABOUT 16 SERVINGS

1 pound boneless salmon filet with skin

1 tablespoon vegetable oil

¼ teaspoon salt, plus more to taste

⅛ teaspoon freshly ground pepper, plus more to taste

½ pound sliced smoked salmon

2 scallions, white and green parts, chopped

6 tablespoons (¾ stick) unsalted butter, cut into pieces

2 tablespoons heavy cream

Chopped scallion greens, for garnish

Assorted fresh vegetables, such as celery sticks, cucumber slices, carrots, cherry tomatoes, broccoli and cauliflower florets, Belgian endive and fennel sticks, for serving

For a charcoal grill, build a fire and burn until coals are covered in white ash. For a gas grill, preheat to high. Oil grill grate.

Brush fish on both sides with oil and season with salt and pepper. Place fish on grill and cover. Grill, flesh side down, until underside is seared with grill marks, about 3 minutes. Turn and grill until flesh looks barely opaque when flaked with the tip of a knife, about 5 minutes more. Transfer to a plate and cool. Remove skin and discard.

Pulse grilled salmon and smoked salmon in a food processor fitted with a metal blade, until chopped. Add scallions. With machine running, add butter, 1 piece at a time. Add cream and process until smooth. Season with salt and pepper. Scrape into a serving bowl and cover. Refrigerate to blend flavors, at least 1 hour. (The spread can be prepared, covered and refrigerated, up to 2 days ahead.)

Arrange vegetables, with bowl of salmon spread, on a platter. Supply small knives to help apply spread onto vegetables.

Sweet and spicy meatballs

Lilly spices up her meatballs with jalapeño jelly and Dijon mustard, but this crowd-pleaser works with almost any sauce you can concoct. If you aren't in the mood to make the meatballs (which Lilly isn't most of the time), pick up a big bag of frozen ones from "the club" (Sam's, BJ's, Costco and so on).

16 TO 20 PARTY SERVINGS

MEATBALLS

3 pounds ground round

1 cup Italian seasoned dried bread crumbs

3 large eggs, beaten

1 large onion, minced

½ cup chopped parsley

4 garlic cloves, pushed through garlic press

1 tablespoon salt

1 teaspoon freshly ground pepper

SWEET AND SPICY SAUCE

2 tablespoons extra-virgin olive oil

1 medium onion, finely chopped

One 8-ounce jar jalapeño jelly

One 12-ounce bottle chili sauce

½ cup grape jelly

2 tablespoons soy sauce

1 tablespoon Dijon mustard

Position racks in center and top third of the oven and preheat oven to 400°F. Lightly oil two baking sheets.

To make meatballs, combine beef, bread crumbs, eggs, onion, parsley, garlic, salt and pepper in a large bowl. Mix until well combined. Using 1 tablespoon for each, roll into balls and place on baking sheets. You will have about 75 meatballs. Bake until browned, about 20 minutes. (The meatballs can be made, and then cooled, stored in plastic bags and refrigerated for up to 2 days or frozen for up to 1 month. If frozen, thaw before cooking in the sauce.)

To make sauce, heat oil in a large saucepan over medium heat. Add onion and cook, stirring occasionally, until golden, about 5 minutes. Stir in jalapeño jelly, chili sauce, grape jelly, soy sauce and mustard and bring to a boil. Reduce heat under sauce to low. Stir in meatballs and cover. Cook, stirring often, until meatballs are heated through, about 10 minutes (20 minutes if meatballs are chilled).

To serve, transfer meatballs to an ignited chafing dish and serve hot.

El grande Cuban sandwich

A hot and crusty stuffed sandwich is a great, informal way to feed a crowd. If your delicatessen carries roast pork, substitute one-and-a-quarter pounds sliced pork for the freshly roasted pork tenderloin.

2 LARGE SANDWICHES, ABOUT 12 SERVINGS EACH

1 pork tenderloin, about 1¼ pounds

1 teaspoon dried thyme

½ teaspoon salt

¼ teaspoon freshly ground pepper

2 tablespoons extra-virgin olive oil

¼ cup mayonnaise

2 tablespoons Dijon mustard

Two 15-inch-long, soft-crusted bread loaves, unsliced

10 ounces sliced Swiss cheese

8 ounces sliced ham

24 dill pickle slices

Vegetable oil spray, for the aluminum foil

Position rack in center of oven and preheat to 400°F.

Using a thin, sharp knife, trim silver skin from pork. Fold back pointed ends and tie with kitchen string. Rub tenderloin with thyme, salt and pepper. Heat oil in a large ovenproof skillet over medium-high heat and sear tenderloin on all sides, about 5 minutes. Place skillet in oven and roast until an instant-read meat thermometer inserted in center of meat reaches 150°F, about 25 minutes. Cool completely. (The tenderloin can be roasted up to 1 day ahead, and then cooled, covered and refrigerated.)

Position rack in center of oven and preheat to 400°F. Place two large baking sheets in oven to heat.

Split each loaf lengthwise. Combine mayonnaise and mustard and spread half on each loaf of bread. Thinly slice tenderloin. Layer equal amounts of sliced pork, Swiss cheese and ham on bottom halves of both loaves, and top with dill pickle slices. Cover with top halves.

Spray a large sheet of aluminum foil with vegetable oil. Wrap 1 loaf, sprayed side in. Repeat with second loaf. Place loaves on 1 heated baking sheet. Top with second hot baking sheet, weighed down with an ovenproof skillet. Bake until crust is toasty (open foil to check), about 25 minutes.

Let loaves stand at room temperature for 5 minutes. Unwrap and slice crosswise into 1½-inch-wide pieces with a serrated knife. Transfer to a serving platter and serve warm.

Roasted pumpkin salsa with tortilla chips

Pumpkin equals Halloween, so it's fun to include it on your party's menu. If you want to use true pumpkin, it must be a cooking variety, such as sugar or cheese, not the watery Jack O' Lantern type. Butternut squash or calabasa (found at Latino grocers) are great substitutes. Putting pumpkin in salsa may sound like a stretch, but pumpkin is actually savory, and the result is a spicy and colorful dip for tortilla chips. Create a bowl for the salsa by hollowing out the best-looking pumpkin in the patch.

ABOUT 2 QUARTS, 16 TO 24 PARTY SERVINGS

3 pounds winter squash, such as sugar or cheese pumpkin, butternut squash or calabasa, pared, seeded and cut in ½-inch chunks

4 tablespoons extra-virgin olive oil, divided

1 large onion, diced

1 large red bell pepper, seeds and ribs discarded, cut into ¼-inch dice

4 garlic cloves, minced

1 jalapeño pepper, seeded and minced

1 tablespoon chili powder

One 28-ounce can diced tomatoes, drained

2 large zucchini, cut into ½-inch dice

3 tablespoons chopped cilantro

¼ cup coarsely chopped shelled and toasted pumpkin seeds (pepitas)

Tortilla chips, for serving

Position rack in center of oven and preheat oven to 400°F. Lightly oil a baking sheet.

Toss squash with 2 tablespoons oil and spread on baking sheet. Roast, stirring occasionally, until lightly browned and tender, about 25 minutes.

Meanwhile, heat remaining 2 tablespoons oil in a large saucepan over medium-high heat. Add onion, red pepper, garlic and jalapeño, and cook, stirring occasionally, until onion is golden, about 8 minutes. Stir in chili powder. Add tomatoes, zucchini and cilantro, and cook, stirring occasionally, until zucchini is crisp-tender, about 5 minutes. Stir in roasted squash and cook for 5 additional minutes to blend flavors. Cool completely. (The salsa can be made, and then cooled, covered and refrigerated, up to 3 days ahead. Remove from the refrigerator 1 hour before serving.)

Transfer to a serving bowl (or a hallowed-out pumpkin) and serve at room temperature with tortilla chips, and pepitas on the side.

Halloween sugar cookies

While most people save a project like this for Christmas, what's to keep you from decorating cookies cut out in Halloween designs? The royal icing, which dries hard and shiny, will give your cookies a professional-looking sheen. For the brightest colors, use food coloring paste instead of liquid. You local bakery or supermarket is bound to have some good-looking cookies if homemade cookies aren't in the cards.

ABOUT 3 ½ DOZEN, DEPENDING ON SIZE

COOKIES

3 cups all-purpose flour

1½ teaspoons baking powder

½ teaspoon salt

12 tablespoons (1½ sticks) unsalted butter, at room temperature

1 cup granulated sugar

2 large eggs, beaten

1½ teaspoons vanilla extract

ROYAL ICING

1 pound (4½ cups) confectioner's sugar

2 tablespoons dried egg white powder (available at natural food stores and most supermarkets)

6 tablespoons water

Food coloring paste (available at kitchenware shops) or liquid, as desired

Small icing spatula, for decorating cookies

Position racks in top and bottom thirds of oven and preheat oven to 350ºF.

Sift flour, baking powder and salt together. Beat butter and sugar in a large bowl with an electric mixer on high speed (a heavy-duty standing mixer with the paddle blade works best) until pale and fluffy, about 3 minutes. One at a time, beat in eggs, then vanilla. On low speed, beat in flour mixture just until combined. Gather up dough, divide into two thick discs and wrap each in plastic wrap. Refrigerate until chilled, about 1½ hours. (The dough can be prepared up to 1 day ahead.)

To roll out cookies, work with one disc at a time, keeping the other disc refrigerated. Remove dough from refrigerator and let stand at room temperature until just warm enough to roll out without cracking, 5 to 10 minutes. (If the dough has been chilled for longer than 1½ hours, it will take longer.) Place dough on a lightly floured work surface and dust top of dough with flour. Roll out dough to ⅛- to ¼-inch thickness. Using cookie cutters, cut out cookies and transfer to ungreased cookie sheets, placing the cookies 1 inch apart. Gently knead the scraps together and form into another disc. Wrap and chill for 5 minutes before rolling out again to cut out more cookies. Repeat to use all dough.

Bake, switching position of sheets from top to bottom and front to back halfway into baking, until the edges of the cookies are golden, about 10 minutes. Cool on sheets for 2 minutes, then transfer to wire cooling racks to cool completely.

To make icing, combine confectioner's sugar, dried egg whites and water in bowl of heavy-duty standing mixer fitted with paddle blade. Mix on high speed until icing is thick and shiny, about 5 minutes.

Divide icing between small bowls or disposable plastic cups, and tint as desired with food coloring paste. When not using, keep icing covered tightly with plastic wrap to avoid drying out. Decorate cookies as desired. To spread even areas of color, thin icing with drops of water until icing is about the consistency of heavy cream. Use a small icing spatula to spread icing on cookies. To pipe designs, thin icing with drops of water until icing is about the consistency of thick glue. Place icing in small plastic bag, snip off corner with scissors and pipe designs as desired. Place decorated cookies on wire cake racks to set icing. (The cookies can be prepared up to 3 days ahead, and then stored in airtight containers at room temperature.)

NOTE: For Halloween cookie cutters, try coppergifts.com or confectionaryhouse.com.

LILLY'S BIRTHDAY

"I'd love to have ox tongue, but I'm the only one who eats it. No one else would come."

—LILLY, ON PLANNING HER
BIRTHDAY SUPPER MENU

There have been parties galore at Lilly's, but some of the very best are the small suppers sitting at the table in her kitchen. It's a wonderful room—the true soul of her house—with restaurant-quality appliances and enough dinnerware and table linens to stock a small hotel. Yet the effect is cozy rather than intimidating, the look lived-in rather than there just for show. If Lilly asks you to get something from one of the two sub-zero refrigerators, she'll say, "Grab it out of the icebox." Each item in her kitchen, from the smallest ceramic eggcup to the largest roasting pan, is there for a reason: it's in constant use.

The big round table, with its Lazy Susan and shocking pink chairs, sits off to the side in a recessed bay and is firmly anchored by a wildly colorful banquette. On one side, tall sliders face the pool; from the other, you can witness all the action at "command central," the large workstation where Lilly turns out creations as gastronomically delicious as her Lilly dresses are visually mouthwatering.

For a woman who once said, "Mother—boil an egg? I don't think she even knew where the kitchen was." However, Lilly, as well as her sister Flo, have both turned into exceptional cooks. They both would scoff at any praise, but as their friend Petie Reed declares, "These girls are pretty good in the kitchen, I must say."

Every year on Lilly's birthday, Lilly, her family and her close friends gather around a table for a simple meal of home-cooked food.

"When we were young," Lilly remembers, "our birthday parties were always the same—chicken hash, rice and peas. For dessert there were individual ice cream molds shaped like flowers and a birthday cake with little wrapped-up favors baked in it.

Birthday supper

PÂTÉ WITH GREEN BEAN SALAD

CHICKEN POT PIES WITH
PUFF PASTRY CRUST

CHOCOLATE-RASPBERRY
TRUFFLE CAKE

"We would have our friends over and wear our party dresses—the same ones we'd wear to dancing class. Everyone wore patent leather Mary Janes with white socks, except for us. We had to wear bronze slippers. I don't know why. At the time we hated them because they weren't like everybody else's.

"As teenagers, my older sister, Memsie, didn't like parties, but I did. Flo was going through her shy stage. We'd have little dances and things like that, with a band playing, and records, too.

"I remember one party vividly because we screamed about it for years (after we got over being totally embarrassed). It was a dance and, as mononucleosis was big then, Mother kept insisting, 'No kissing allowed.' But naturally nobody listened to her.

"Ogden, my stepfather, had a wicked sense of humor; in the middle of the party he donned a miner's lamp on his head, grabbed a pitchfork and went outside, stamping through the underbrush. All the kissing couples were ordered back to the dance floor. As the kids say now, what a bummer! Mother kept insisting it was because of mononucleosis. Sure!"

Lilly's Palm Beach birthday parties were festive and fun. They were perhaps not on the level of Enrique's—"His were the best, the ultimate"—but even Lilly put on a costume now and then. There was her famous Cowboys and Indians Party, celebrating a joint birthday for herself and her friend Alina Farinas.

"Teepees were erected on the lawn and bales of hay plopped everywhere," Lilly says. "I think we had a hokey band with banjoes and guitars and a great fortune-teller in one of the teepees. Picnic tables and horseless wagons completed the decor. Alina and I were killer squaws with humongous headdresses."

Nowadays, birthdays are again what they once were: simple dinners with a cake. The eagerly anticipated cake comes from Annie Van Durand, Lilly's close friend and former next door neighbor, and is fondly known as "VD's Sliding Polish Cake." It's a concoction of "cake, meringue, chocolate, raspberries, nuts, jam, guava, more chocolate and I'm sure a bottle of booze. We're always waiting for it to explode when we light the candles. It truly defies description. It's highly decorated and is constantly sliding off the tray. It's my favorite," declares Lilly.

Sitting around her table fills you with a sense of delightful anticipation. You know something special is going to happen. Each place is set with Matisse-inspired place mats and big square napkins that look like cabbage roses sitting in your wineglass. The Lazy Susan has a candle or three or four, an orchid plant or two, and all these wonderful chutneys and condiments that only Lilly seems to know about. Dinner is served buffet style, so everyone helps themselves and takes a seat. There are no place cards here, but there is that one chair festooned with balloons and streamers, waiting for the birthday girl.

"Hurry up and sit down," one guest will urge, "before you get another year older!"

With a smile—and a quick snap of a dish towel at that cheeky guest—she'll do just that.

What to get Lilly for her birthday?

"It ain't easy, honey, let me tell you," admits Lilly's friend Susanna Cutts. "This is a woman who, almost literally, has everything." And it's true. Lilly does have many things, but things aren't anywhere near as important to her as her peeps. A phone call, a smile, a hug, a kiss, a wave—these are gifts that she treasures as much if not more than anything in one of those pale blue boxes from Tiffany's.

If you want to go the tangible route, however, here are some thoughts:

Remember, no candles or scented soaps. They're the cop-out gifts. However, chocolate is a guilty pleasure that's always welcomed.

"You can't go wrong if you give her something for the jungle," advises her friend Denis La Marsh, a.k.a. "Doll." Lilly has a big ceramic turtle by the pool and a cement alligator that's "very happy living in my riverbed," Lilly says.

A really good thriller or mystery. Lilly's a voracious reader, but the book must be current as she gets them fresh off the presses.

A donation to a local animal shelter is the best gift as it's a way to help a cause close to Lilly's heart.

Lilly's most memorable birthday
(and it wasn't even her own!)

"My friend Franci Dixon was married to an Air Force general, Bill Young. Joan Fontaine, who was married to his brother for what seemed like 10 minutes, gave him the nickname "General Honey." We all adored this man. He was elegant, funny and very bright. Our three kids and their three all went to school together, and were the same ages and best friends.

A group of us pretty-young-things formed the General Honey's Youth Movement. We had T-shirts made with his name in a circle of Latin script. General Honey set the cutoff age at 32, so Franci and her friend Nancy White, who was the editor of *Harper's Bazaar*, couldn't be members, as they were just over the age limit.

One year for his birthday we decided to give him a big party. We hired an old fire engine, covered it with yellow asters and had a director's chair for General Honey. It was his throne. We paraded up Seaview and down Seaspray. Quite spectacular. His bevy of loyal fans, plus the children, plus a Dixieland band were all hanging over the engine. The dogs were barking and going bananas.

When we finally hit their house, Villa Vanilla, we sounded like a five-alarm fire! General Honey only allowed members of the Youth Movement to come to the party! No one else was admitted. The two advisors, Nancy White and Franci, could come in and clear the dishes, but that was it.

General Honey had a blast. Everyone had so much fun. I had a ball. It was a magnificent day, proving once again that it is in giving that we receive, for I've never enjoyed a birthday more."

Pâté with green bean salad

Your neighborhood gourmet shop (or perhaps your local supermarket) will have a selection of different pâtés. Choose your favorite, or even a couple to serve as an assortment, and you're on your way to a simple first course. Offer crusty French baguette slices, grainy mustard and tiny cornichons on the side.

8 SERVINGS

1 pound green beans, trimmed and cut into 1-inch lengths

1½ tablespoons red wine vinegar

2 tablespoons finely chopped shallots

1 teaspoon Dijon mustard

½ cup extra-virgin olive oil

Salt and freshly ground pepper, to taste

1 pound store-bought pâté, cut into 8 individual portions

Baguette slices, whole-grain mustard and cornichons, for serving

Bring a large saucepan of lightly salted water to a boil over high heat. Add green beans and cook until bright green and barely tender, 3 to 4 minutes. Drain, rinse under cold water and drain again. Pat dry on paper towels. (The green beans can be prepared 1 day ahead, and then wrapped in fresh paper towels, stored in a plastic bag and refrigerated.)

Whisk vinegar, shallots and Dijon in a small bowl. Gradually whisk in oil. Season with salt and pepper. (The vinaigrette can be prepared 1 day ahead, and then covered and refrigerated. Whisk to recombine.)

About 1 hour before serving, remove pâté from refrigerator so it can lose its chill. When ready to serve, toss green beans and vinaigrette in a medium bowl, and season again with salt and pepper. Place each portion of pâté on a plate, with a mound of green bean salad next to pâté. Serve immediately, with bread, mustard and cornichons.

Chicken pot pies with puff pastry crust

Is there a more comforting, satisfying supper entrée than homemade chicken pot pie? Lilly's recipe for creamed chicken gets plenty of use in her kitchen. With a few minor alterations, it becomes chicken hash to serve over waffles for Christmas brunch. The recipe may seem lengthy, but it is really simple. You will need eight 14- to 16-ounce ramekins or ovenproof soup bowls (such as French onion soup bowls), available at kitchenware shops. 8 SERVINGS

CHICKEN FILLING

1 roaster chicken (about 6½ pounds), cut into 2 each drumsticks, wings, breasts and wings, neck and giblets reserved

1 large onion, chopped

1 large celery rib, chopped

4 sprigs fresh parsley

¼ teaspoon dried thyme

¼ teaspoon whole black peppercorns

2 cups half-and-half

4 tablespoons (½ stick) unsalted butter

¼ cup all-purpose flour

2 tablespoons dry sherry, such as Tio Pepe

½ teaspoon freshly grated nutmeg

One 12-ounce package frozen mixed vegetables (corn, green beans, carrots and lima beans), thawed

1½ cups frozen whole boiling onions, thawed

1 tablespoon chopped fresh tarragon or 1½ teaspoons dried tarragon

Salt and freshly ground pepper, to taste

One 17-ounce package frozen puff pastry sheets, thawed overnight in the refrigerator

1 large egg, beaten

To make filling, combine chicken, including neck and giblets (but not liver), onion and celery in a large soup pot and add enough cold water to cover chicken by 1 inch. Bring to a boil over high heat, skimming off foam that rises to surface. Add parsley, thyme and peppercorns. Reduce heat to medium-low. Simmer until chicken shows no sign of pink when pierced with tip of a knife, about 1 hour. Strain through a colander into a large bowl. Reserve 2 cups chicken broth, and save remaining broth for another use. Cool chicken until easy to handle. Discard skin and bones and chop chicken meat into bite-size pieces.

Heat chicken broth and half-and-half in a medium saucepan (or microwave oven) until hot. Melt butter in a large saucepan over medium heat. Whisk in flour and reduce heat to low. Let bubble without browning for 2 minutes. Whisk in hot broth mixture, sherry and nutmeg, and bring to a boil over medium heat, whisking often. Return heat to low and simmer, whisking often, until sauce is smooth and lightly thickened, about 10 minutes. Stir in chicken, mixed vegetables, onions and tarragon. Season with salt and pepper. (The chicken filling can be prepared up to 1 day ahead, and then cooled, covered and refrigerated. Reheat gently before serving.)

Position rack in center and top third of oven and preheat oven to 400°F.

Roll out 1 pastry sheet on a lightly floured surface just to remove creases in dough. Cut out 4 rounds of dough, 1 inch larger than diameter of ramekin. (Pastry rounds can be prepared 4 hours ahead, and then covered and refrigerated.)

For each serving, spoon equal amounts of chicken mixture into the eight 14- to 16-ounce ramekins or deep ovenproof soup bowls. Brush edge of each ramekin or bowl with egg. Place pastry on top of ramekin or bowl, stretching pastry taut and pressing firmly around edges to be sure it adheres to ramekin or bowl. Lightly brush top of pastry with egg.

Place ramekins or bowls on two baking sheets. Bake, switching positions of baking sheets from top to bottom halfway through baking, until tops are puffed and golden brown, about 20 minutes. Serve immediately.

CHICKEN HASH: Make chicken pot pie filling, but delete sherry, mixed vegetables and onions. Substitute 2 tablespoons chopped fresh parsley for tarragon. When filling is thickened, beat 4 large egg yolks in a medium bowl. Stir in 2 cups sauce, and return to simmering sauce in saucepan. Stir in chicken and cook, stirring often, just until chicken is heated through. Do not boil, or yolks could curdle. Serve hot.

Chocolate-raspberry truffle cake

This dense, fudgy flourless chocolate cake is all about the chocolate, so be sure to use the best you can find. Do be careful that the cacao content (now listed on many brands) isn't above sixty-five percent, or your bittersweet cake could be too bitter. Plan on baking and chilling the cake one day ahead so it can firm up, then warming it just before serving. The Whipped Cream makes it that much more delish.

10 TO 12 SERVINGS

12 tablespoons (1½ sticks) unsalted butter, cut up

1 pound high-quality bittersweet chocolate, chopped

4 large eggs, separated, at room temperature

¼ cup granulated sugar

Three ½-pint cartons fresh raspberries, divided

Whipped Cream (recipe follows)

Position rack in center of oven and preheat oven to 350°F. Lightly butter and flour an 8 inch springform pan, tapping out excess flour.

Melt butter in a medium saucepan over medium heat. Remove from heat and add chocolate. Let stand until chocolate softens, about 5 minutes, then whisk until smooth. One at a time, whisk in yolks.

Beat whites in a clean medium bowl with an electric mixer on low speed until whites are foamy. Increase mixer to high and beat just until whites form soft peaks. One tablespoon at a time, beat in granulated sugar, just until peaks are stiff and shiny, but not dry. Stir about one-fourth of beaten whites into chocolate mixture, then pour over whites and fold in. Fold in ½ pint of raspberries. Spread evenly in pan.

Bake just until edges are puffed and set, but center still looks unset, 25 to 30 minutes.

Cool completely on a wire cake rack. Run a sharp knife around inside of pan to release cake from sides. Wrap cake in plastic wrap and refrigerate overnight. (The cake can be made up to 2 days ahead, and then covered and refrigerated.)

Remove cake from refrigerator 1 hour before serving. Place cake on a serving platter and top with remaining raspberries. Cut cake into wedges with a sharp knife dipped in hot water and transfer to dessert plates. Add a large dollop of Whipped Cream to each. Serve immediately.

WHIPPED CREAM: Combine ¾ cup heavy cream, 2 tablespoons confectioner's sugar and 1 teaspoon vanilla extract in a chilled medium bowl. Beat with an electric mixer on high speed until stiff. (The cream can be whipped 8 hours ahead, and then covered and refrigerated. If it separates, whisk to recombine.)

THANKSGIVING

*"Come for Thanksgiving,
and bring your bathing suit.
Not two things you often hear
in the same sentence."*

—NANCY "NA-NA" KEZELE, LILLY'S FRIEND

illy has one basic secret when it comes to Thanksgiving—well, really, to cooking in general: "Take every shortcut that is known to man." It's a good thing, too, as those giving thanks in Lilly's slat house tend to number upward of thirty-some people. It's the usual mix of family and friends, or, as Lilly says, "It's the same every year except for the ones who've croaked, or when a new face hits town."

One thing she does, which sets a lot of purists' teeth on edge—much to her amusement—is roast her turkeys a week or so in advance of Thanksgiving, and then freeze them, sliced and covered in their own broth. "With all those people coming," she asks, "who wants to be stuck carving four or five turkeys at zero hour? I pull mine out of the oven, throw my stuffing under them and add some gravy, and it's perfect."

The broth that Lilly makes from the turkey carcass and then uses to drown the fresh sliced turkey as it freezes keeps it nice and moist.

Flo will do a small bird for show, if anyone has a special hankering for a drumstick. Lilly boasts, "It works like a Thanksgiving morning dream, except for the year when, knowing all this delicious turkey was sitting in the freezer, we had an impromptu party the week before Thanksgiving and had to repeat the whole process. Couldn't believe we had to 'practice' Thanksgiving!"

In that elegant back-slanting handwriting that young ladies of her generation perfected at boarding school, Lilly will write up a simple menu. Her notes for a lunch for thirty include turkey, stuffing, gravy, sausages (only Jones), green beans ("beanies"), onions (Flo's Onions), mashed potatoes ("mashers"), turnip and potato puree, bread, cranberry sauce, cranberry relish (friend Julie McConnell supplies her famous homemade relish) and cider.

No dessert?

"I don't pay too much attention to desserts anymore," Lilly explains. "We always cooked or the guests brought so many. We would end up so stuffed that the goodies would be slammed into the freezer. (Nothing like pumpkin cheesecake in July.) I think what put the damper on a hoard

Thanksgiving, Lilly style

OLD-FASHIONED ROAST TURKEY WITH HOMEMADE GRAVY

LILLY'S MAKE-AHEAD TURKEY

LOTS AND LOTS OF JONES SAUSAGES

SAUSAGE AND DRIED FRUIT STUFFING

FLO'S ONIONS

JULIE'S CRANBERRY RELISH

INDULGENT MASHED POTATOES

LILLY'S LEGENDARY POTATO-TURNIP PUREE

GREEN BEAN AND BACON SAUTÉ

GINGERED PUMPKIN TART

of sweeties was when my darling friend Sandi brought the pecan pie from hell that she had slaved over, complete with burnt top and totally dried out. Basta! Enough! Now we're down to miniature Dove bars and two pies."

A couple of items on the menu are family favorites. Amy Pulitzer, Lilly's daughter-in-law from California, says, "A huge thing about Thanksgiving is Lilly's famous potato and turnip puree. I never see it anyplace else and everyone rebels against me if I try to make it at home as no one makes it quite the way she does.

"And the sausages. The turkeys are always surrounded by Jones sausages. There seem to be four pounds of sausages for every one pound of turkey.

"Last year they had ten dozen—does that tell you how this family feels about saucisson?"

Then there are Flo's Onions, a savory delight that starts with a jar of Aunt Nellie's bottled onions. Flo's Onions are so good that one year Liza, who was living in England, called across the Atlantic for the recipe. Lilly complied in the way that she, and only she, shares a recipe, including the "big glug of sherry" and the "nice plop of Dijon mustard." She also told Liza to use bottled onions. Liza did. Tiny cocktail onions—four hundred of them. The recipe didn't quite taste the same. It's a story they still laugh about.

Thanksgiving lunch is on the early side—1:30. "Anything later wastes the whole day." And, indeed, people are invited to bring their bathing suits. "We're in and out of the pool all day."

"As always, lunch is served buffet style," Lilly says. "The tables last year were decorated with chocolate turkeys and foul-smelling plastic-coated autumn leaves. We even went as far as to having paper plates (Chinette), and the larger paper cups were green and red. We were elegant enough to have beautiful napkins and assorted silverware—some red, some silver. How easy is that? The cooked turkey and the throwaway plates. What a great Thanksgiving. Cleanup took six minutes!"

Now let's get serious and talk about the day after. The options are unlimited: sandwiches or wraps; stuffing and cranberry; turkey and stuffing, spewing forth with mayo; sausage and stuffing, with cranberry; hot turkey, with gravy or string beans, and diced turkey, with French dressing.

"The unfortunate thing is that the day after we usually have nothing left," Lilly says. "We have gotten into the habit of giving it all away after lunch. The peeps all want leftovers, so we divvy up what's left. Everyone goes home with bulging Ziplocks. They wake up with heavy-on-the-mayo goodies, and we're back to granola!"

The night before the big day

With so much going on Thanks-giving Eve—all the preparations and the kids coming home from school and college—the last thing you need to worry about is what to have for din-ner. With all the food that's about to be consumed, a light and easy menu is called for, and Lilly has the perfect one: scallops wrapped in bacon and served on a bed of steamed spinach. You can whip it up yourself or, as Lilly says, "Why bother? Pick it up at Costco." Like that old Burt Bacharach song says, "Make it easy on yourself."

The Pilly-grims and the Hindy-ans

Enrique loved to give a Thanksgiving toast. Although his mellifluous Cuban accent massacred the story of the first Thanksgiving, it was a heartfelt, if hilari-ous, tribute nonetheless. Lilly remem-bers, "One year everyone had to wear either a bonnet—and be a 'Pilly-grim'—or a feather—and be a 'Hindy-an'. He loved to give those toasts and we were always cracking up."

The best Thanksgiving movies

After a big dinner—if you don't have a pool, and you can't work up the energy for step-aerobics—go ahead, be a flopper and just watch one of these great Thanksgiving movies.

Home for the Holidays Holly Hunter, Robert Downey Jr., Anne Bancroft and Charles Durning in this spot-on look at a functioning dysfunctional family who gather for Thanksgiving. Directed by Jodie Foster.

Planes, Trains & Automobiles Steve Martin will do anything to get home to his family for Thanksgiving, even hitch a ride with John Candy.

Dutch A John Hughes comedy about a bonding trip between an obnox-ious 12-year-old prep school boy and his mother's blue-collar boyfriend.

Hannah and Her Sisters Certainly Woody Allen's warmest and one of his funniest romantic comedies, bracketed around a pair of family Thanksgivings.

Flo's "week in review"

Flo's "week in review" soup is famous in the family. She literally takes whatever's leftover in her icebox, heats it up, throws it in a blender and purees it into a thick, delicious soup.

"Sauté an onion and a little garlic in a bottom of a pot," Flo explains, "and then start tossing stuff in…gravy…onions…salad…everything you've got. Stir it around until it gets nice and ten-der, then transfer it ladle by ladle to a blender and puree it into a nice, thick consistency. It's fantastic."

Old-fashioned roast turkey with homemade gravy

Here's how to roast a golden brown, moist bird that will look just like the one photographed on the cover of a food magazine. Nobody likes dry turkey meat. Protecting the breast area with foil will help keep that trouble area nice and juicy. Don't skip making the Turkey Stock, as it will add incredible flavor to the gravy. If you choose not to stuff the bird, add a sliced onion or a couple of chopped celery ribs to the body cavity. ABOUT 12 SERVINGS

One 18-pound turkey, neck and giblets reserved for Turkey Stock, rinsed and patted dry

Sausage and Dried Fruit Stuffing (page 144), as needed

8 tablespoons (1 stick) unsalted butter, softened

Salt and freshly ground black pepper, to taste

8 cups Turkey Stock (recipe follows), as needed

½ cup all-purpose flour

Position rack in bottom third of oven and preheat oven to 325°F. Loosely fill reserved turkey neck with some Sausage and Dried Fruit Stuffing. Using a wooden or metal skewer, pin neck skin to back skin. Fold turkey wings akimbo behind back or tie to body with kitchen string. Loosely fill body cavity with more stuffing. Place any remaining stuffing in a lightly buttered baking dish, and then cover and refrigerate to bake as a side dish. Place drumsticks in hock lock or tie together with kitchen string.

Place turkey on a rack in a large flameproof roasting pan. Rub all over with butter and season with salt and pepper. Roast, basting every hour with juices in pan (lift up foil to reach breast), until a meat thermometer inserted in meaty part of thigh (but not touching a bone) reads 180°F and stuffing is at least 160°F, about 5 hours, 45 minutes. Whenever pan drippings look dry, add 2 cups Turkey Stock or water to pan. Remove foil during last hour of roasting to allow skin to brown. Transfer turkey to a large serving platter and let stand at least 20 minutes before carving.

Meanwhile, pour drippings from roasting pan into a heat-proof glass bowl or measuring cup. Let stand 5 minutes, then skim off rendered fat that rises to surface; reserve ½ cup fat. Add enough Turkey Stock to drippings to measure 6 cups.

Place roasting pan over two burners on medium heat and add reserved turkey fat. Whisk in flour, scraping up browned bits on bottom of pan, and cook uncovered until lightly browned, about 2 minutes. Whisk in broth mixture, bring to a boil and reduce heat to medium-low. Cook, whisking often, until gravy thickens, about 10 minutes. Season with salt and pepper. Transfer gravy to a sauceboat. Carve turkey and serve with gravy.

TURKEY STOCK: Brown 3 pounds turkey wings, chopped between joints with a heavy knife, in 1 tablespoon vegetable oil in a large stockpot over medium-high heat. (If you have made Lilly's Make-Ahead Turkey on page 144, substitute the roasted turkey carcass and skin for wings, breaking up carcass to fit pot, and do not brown.) Add 1 medium onion, 1 medium carrot and 1 medium celery rib, all chopped, and cook until softened, about 5 minutes. Add turkey neck and giblets (but not liver) and enough cold water to cover wings (or carcass) by 1 inch. Bring to a boil over high heat, scraping up browned bits in pot and skimming off foam on surface. Add 3 parsley sprigs, ¼ teaspoon dried thyme, 6 whole black peppercorns and 1 small bay leaf. Reduce heat to low and simmer for 3 hours (2 hours if using roasted turkey carcass). Strain into a large bowl. Cool to room temperature. Cover and refrigerate overnight. Scrape off hardened fat from surface. Reheat in a large saucepan before using. (The stock can be prepared up to 3 days ahead, and then cooled, covered and refrigerated, or frozen for up to 3 months.)

Lilly's make-ahead turkey

Lilly always has a crowd for Thanksgiving, and gets her turkey roasting done way ahead of time so she's not stuck carving as everyone's coming in the door. Frozen turkey can dry out, but Lilly's trick is to cover it with homemade Turkey Stock before freezing. If you wish, use the carcass to make the Turkey Stock.

ABOUT 12 SERVINGS

Old-Fashioned Roast Turkey (page 143)

4 cups Turkey Stock (page 143), as needed

Follow instructions for Old-Fashioned Roast Turkey through transfering turkey to a large platter. Carve turkey; reserve carcass and skin for Turkey Stock, if desired.

Cool turkey completely. Layer equal amounts of carved turkey in two 9 X 13-inch disposable aluminum baking pans. Add enough Turkey Stock to barely cover turkey and cool stock. Cover tightly with plastic wrap and then wrap with aluminum foil. Freeze for up to 1 month. Make gravy at this stage and also freeze.

The night before serving, defrost turkey overnight in refrigerator. Position racks in center and top third of oven and preheat oven to 350°F. To reheat, remove plastic wrap and foil. Pour off about half of turkey stock from each pan (reserve for gravy, if desired). Cover again with foil and bake until stock is steaming and turkey is heated through, about 40 minutes. Serve hot.

Sausage and dried fruit stuffing

Lilly likes a stuffing with lots of flavors, such as this winner with dried apricots, dried plums, pork sausage and fresh herbs. Never make stuffing the night before; chilled stuffing takes too long to heat up inside of the turkey. To save time, sauté the sausage and vegetables on Wednesday night, then heat them through in a skillet before making the stuffing on Thursday morning. 10 TO 12 SERVINGS

1 pound sage-flavored bulk pork sausage

8 tablespoons (1 stick) unsalted butter

1 large onion, chopped

3 ribs celery, cut into ¼-inch-thick slices

One 16-ounce bag seasoned stuffing cubes

⅔ cup dried plums, cut into quarters

⅔ cup dried apricots, cut into quarters

¼ cup chopped parsley

1 tablespoon fresh or 2 teaspoons dried rosemary

1 tablespoon fresh or 2 teaspoons dried sage

½ teaspoon freshly ground pepper

2 cups Turkey Stock (page 143) or chicken broth

Cook sausage in a large skillet over medium heat, breaking up with a spoon, until it shows no sign of pink, about 10 minutes. Using a slotted spoon, transfer sausage to a large bowl; leave fat in skillet.

Add butter to sausage fat in skillet and melt. Add onion and celery and cook, stirring occasionally until vegetables are tender, about 10 minutes. Transfer to sausage. Add bread stuffing mix, dried plums and apricots, parsley, rosemary, sage and pepper and mix. Stir in broth to evenly moisten stuffing mix. Use as a stuffing or spread in buttered 15 X 10-inch baking dish and cover with buttered aluminum foil. (If baking in the dish, stuffing can be prepared up to 8 hours ahead, and then covered and refrigerated.)

Position rack in center of oven and preheat to 350ºF. Bake until stuffing is heated through, about 30 minutes. For crusty stuffing, remove foil after 20 minutes and increase oven temperature to 375ºF.

Flo's onions

Flo makes these every year as her contribution to the feast. She prefers Aunt Nellie's bottled onions, but if you can't find them, any white onion will do. Just steer clear of the cocktail or frozen variety!

10 TO 12 SERVINGS

5 tablespoons unsalted butter, divided

4 tablespoons all-purpose flour

1 cup chicken broth

½ cup half-and-half

Four 15-ounce jars whole white boiling onions, drained and rinsed

1½ cups (6 ounces) freshly grated Parmesan cheese

2 tablespoons dry sherry, such as Tio Pepe

1 tablespoon Dijon mustard

1 tablespoon Worcestershire sauce

Salt and freshly ground pepper, to taste

Position rack in center of oven and preheat oven to 375°F. Butter a 9 X 13-inch baking dish.

Melt 4 tablespoons of butter in a medium saucepan over medium-low heat. Whisk in flour. Let bubble without browning for 2 minutes. Whisk in broth and half-and-half. Bring to a simmer and reduce heat to low. Cook, whisking often, until lightly thickened, about 5 minutes. Remove from heat. Stir in onions, 1 cup of Parmesan, sherry, mustard, Worcestershire sauce, salt and pepper. Spread in baking dish. Sprinkle remaining ½ cup Parmesan on top and dot with remaining 1 tablespoon butter. (The onions can be prepared up to 1 day ahead, and then cooled, covered and refrigerated.)

Bake until sauce is bubbling throughout and top is golden brown, about 25 minutes (35 minutes if refrigerated). Serve hot.

Julie's cranberry relish

Lilly's friend Julie has made a specialty of this flavorful side dish. Make it a day or so before Thanksgiving so you don't have to worry about it setting up in time. Be sure to follow Julie's warning about not adding the pineapple to the gelatin mixture until the latter is almost jelled; if added too early, the ring will never set.

10 TO 12 SERVINGS

One 8-ounce can crushed pineapple in juice

½ cup water

2 tablespoons fresh lemon juice

One 3-ounce package raspberry-flavored Jell-O gelatin

One 16-ounce can whole berry cranberry sauce

½ cup diced (¼-inch dice) celery

½ cup coarsely chopped walnuts

Drain pineapple in a wire strainer over a bowl. Press down hard with a spoon to extract ½ cup pineapple juice; reserve pineapple. Bring pineapple juice, water and lemon juice to a boil in a medium saucepan over high heat. Remove from heat and sprinkle in gelatin. Stir constantly for 1 to 2 minutes to completely dissolve gelatin. Add cranberry sauce and stir until sauce around berries dissolves. Pour into a medium bowl set in another bowl of iced water.

Let stand, stirring occasionally, until almost fully jelled (a spoon drawn across the top should leave a swath), about 30 minutes. Stir in drained pineapple, celery and walnuts. Pour into a 5-cup ring mold, and then cover with plastic wrap and refrigerate until firm, at least 4 hours. (The cranberry ring can be made up to 2 days ahead, and then covered and refrigerated.)

To unmold, fill a large bowl with warm water. Dip mold in water for a few seconds, and wipe sides dry with a towel. Press around diameter of ring with thumbs to release from sides of mold, and invert and unmold onto a serving plate. Serve chilled.

Indulgent mashed potatoes

For Thanksgiving, it's not worth making any less than a mountain of mashed potatoes, so Lilly rolls up her sleeves and cooks ten pounds of spuds. The secret ingredient in these fluffy potatoes is a generous amount of mayonnaise stirred in at the end. Don't knock it until you've tried it.

10 TO 12 SERVINGS

10 pounds baking potatoes, such as russets or Burbanks, peeled and cut into 1-inch chunks

1 cup (2 sticks) unsalted butter

1 cup milk, heated, as needed

1 cup mayonnaise

Salt and freshly ground pepper, to taste

Place potatoes in a large stockpot and cover with lightly salted water. Cover and bring to a boil over medium-high heat (allow about 30 minutes). Cook, partially covered, until tender, about 30 minutes. Drain potatoes and return to pot. (Covered tightly, potatoes will stay hot for about 30 minutes before mashing.)

Using a potato masher, mash potatoes and butter. Mash in hot milk a bit at a time until desired consistency is reached. Stir in mayonnaise and season with salt and pepper. If desired, remove 4 cups mashed potatoes for Lilly's Legendary Potato-Turnip Puree. Transfer to a serving bowl and serve hot.

Lilly's legendary potato-turnip puree

These are a required dish at Lilly's Thanksgiving table. Use the large, waxed yellow turnip, also known as rutabaga, and not the white ones with purplish skins. The cooking time varies on the age of the turnip; they can take an hour to simmer to tenderness, so don't be surprised. Turnips can be pureed in a food processor. But don't try this with potatoes or they'll turn gluey.

10 TO 12 SERVINGS

4 pounds waxed yellow turnips (rutabagas), pared with a sharp knife and cut into 1-inch chunks

4 cups Indulgent Mashed Potatoes (see recipe at left)

Salt and freshly ground pepper, to taste

Place turnips in a large stockpot and cover with lightly salted water. Bring to a boil over medium-high heat and cook, partially covered, until tender, about 45 minutes to 1 hour.

Drain turnips. In batches, puree turnips in a food processor fitted with the metal chopping blade and transfer to a medium bowl. Mix in mashed potatoes. Season with salt and pepper. Transfer to a serving bowl and serve hot.

Green bean and bacon sauté

Be sure to include a fresh green vegetable on your Thanksgiving menu. (Mashed potatoes do not count.) Green beans and bacon are old friends, and this quick sauté will be ready in just a few minutes. 12 SERVINGS

2 pounds green beans, trimmed and cut into 1½-inch lengths

8 bacon slices

½ cup Turkey Stock (page 143) or chicken broth

Salt and freshly ground pepper, to taste

Bring a large pot of lightly salted water to a boil over high heat. Add green beans and cook until crisp-tender, about 5 minutes. Drain and rinse under cold water. Pat dry with paper towels. (The green beans can be prepared 1 day ahead, and then wrapped in fresh paper towels, stored in plastic bags and refrigerated.)

Cook bacon in a large skillet over medium-high heat until crisp, about 6 minutes. Transfer bacon to paper towels to drain, leaving fat in skillet. Coarsely chop bacon. (Bacon can be prepared up to 2 hours ahead; leave fat in skillet at room temperature.)

Add beans and Turkey Stock to skillet. Cook, stirring often, until beans are heated through, 3 to 5 minutes. Stir in bacon. Season with salt and pepper. Transfer to a serving dish and serve hot.

Gingered pumpkin tart

Rather than offer an endless array of goodies that never seem to be eaten, Lilly believes that one or two well-chosen desserts will suffice. Try this gingery tart with a delectable shortbread crust that is simply pressed into the tart pan. 8 SERVINGS

CRUST

1¼ **cup all-purpose flour**

2 **tablespoons sugar**

¼ **teaspoon salt**

8 **tablespoons (1 stick) unsalted butter, chilled and cut into 10 slices**

1 **large egg yolk**

FILLING

One 15-ounce can solid-pack pumpkin (1¾ cups)

¾ **cup heavy cream**

¾ **cup packed light brown sugar**

1 **large egg plus 2 large egg yolks, at room temperature, well beaten**

1 **teaspoon ground ginger**

½ **teaspoon ground cinnamon**

Whipped Cream (see recipe page 135), for serving

3 **tablespoons chopped crystallized ginger, for garnish**

Position rack in center of oven and preheat oven to 375°F.

To make crust, pulse flour, sugar and salt in a food processor fitted with a metal chopping blade until combined. Add butter and pulse until mixture resembles coarse cornmeal with a few pea-size chunks of butter. With machine running, add yolk. Pulse just until dough begins to clump together. (If

the dough is dry, add cold water, 1 teaspoon at a time, and pulse until moistened.) Gather up dough.

Press dough firmly and evenly into a 9-inch round tart pan with a removable bottom. Freeze for 15 minutes. Place pan on a baking sheet.

To make filling, whisk pumpkin, cream, brown sugar, egg, yolks, ground ginger and cinnamon in a medium bowl to dissolve sugar. Pour into chilled crust.

Bake for 10 minutes. Reduce oven temperature to 325°F, and continue baking until filling is evenly puffed (the center may seem slightly undercooked), about 50 minutes.

Transfer to a wire cake rack and cool to room temperature. Place pan on a large can, letting side section drop down around can. Cover loosely with plastic wrap and refrigerate until chilled, at least 2 hours. (Tart can be prepared up to 2 days ahead, and then covered and refrigerated.) Serve with a dollop of Whipped Cream and a sprinkle of chopped ginger.

CLOCKWISE FROM TOP LEFT:

Pappy McKim with his three girls, Flossie, Lilly and Memsie, New York City, 1938.

Enrique and Lilly celebrate New Year's Eve at The Coconuts, 1972.

Minnie as an angel (front and center) at Bethesda by the Sea's Christmas pageant, 1960.

Lilly and friend dancing the night away, 1970s.

Winter

"The word 'winter' presents a picture of snow—a long winding driveway,

a toboggan and two Shetland ponies called Pete and Sam,

one black and white, the other gray. We would hitch the toboggan

to the ponies and let them drag it up the big hill.

Then someone would hold them and we would leap on the toboggan for

the long ride down. The holder would then have to plow down the hill,

attach the ponies to the sled and drag us all up again. That went on all day.

Poor holder, poor ponies and three very happy M.M., L.L. and F.F.s."

— LILLY

CHRISTMAS

*"It gets better every year.
There are families within families
within families. Someone always reads
'The Night Before Christmas'
and it's simply magical."*

—SUSANNA CUTTS,
ON CHRISTMAS EVE AT LILLY'S

*C*hristmas in Palm Beach is a pretty amazing sight even if it's not quite the Currier & Ives image that usually comes to mind. Yes, the trees are decorated in twinkling white lights, but they're the palm trees that line Worth Avenue. There is a Christmas parade, but it's a flotilla of boats and pleasure crafts sailing up Lake Worth. And as for Santa? Well, more often than not that portly gent walks right through the front door, as chimneys—with their accompanying fireplaces—are scarce on the horizon.

All of this was a bit of a surprise for Lilly when she first came to live in Palm Beach in the early 1950s. As she recalls, "My first Christmas in Palm Beach was like an experience waiting to happen: Why didn't the temperature drop? Why were the leaves still on the trees and the bougainvillea blooming? I had never been away from cold—sometimes snowing—but always Christmassy Christmases. Too weird.

"The tree looked totally out of place in our rented house—an A-frame with a lot of screens and a pool sparkling in the background. A round fireplace rose in the middle of the living room floor with a hood over it. A fireplace in Palm Beach! For what? I think our first Christmas was spent playing tennis after a morning of ripping and shredding."

Lilly has spent a half century's worth of Christmases in Palm Beach since then, and has adapted to the lack of sledding and mittens. The spirit of Christmas and the bonds of family remain firmly entrenched in her house, and the customary welcoming atmosphere grows warmer given both the season and the lack of chilly weather.

Like most of us, Christmas provides Lilly with a kaleidoscope of happy memories from long ago up through just last year.

"*Y*ears ago, I'd have a big dance on Christmas Eve, with a tent in the backyard. Holy smokes," Lilly says. "I was ambitious then. Enrique liked a Cuban Christmas, which meant roast pork—a huge fresh pork leg that had been marinated for days—lots of fried bananas, black beans, rice and yucca."

The menus

A CUBAN CHRISTMAS EVE DINNER

ROAST PORK LEG WITH CITRUS MARINADE

ZUCCHINI AND GRAPE TOMATOES WITH CILANTRO

YUCCA WITH MOJO

BLACK BEANS AND RICE

TRES LECHES CAKE

CHRISTMAS MORNING BREAKFAST

CHICKEN HASH ON WAFFLES

POMEGRANATE AND PINEAPPLE SALAD

RASPBERRY SUNRISE MIMOSAS

Entering the house as a novice partygoer was an experience in itself. "The first time I came for Christmas," says Susanna, "there was this gigantic tree—the biggest tree I'd ever seen in a private house—covered in these huge tin ornaments from Mexico."

"While I was staying in Nogales with my school buddy Lenny (who was married to the writer Dominick Dunne) I stumbled on these absolutely huge killer decorations," Lilly explains. "Animals, stars and angels—painted on one side and with silvery tin on the other. I must have bought one-hundred-and-fifty of them. This purchase really put a smile on my face. The tree was drop dead and was for a couple of years until the salt air settled in and the little sweethearts were inundated with rust. Too sad."

For many years Liza Pulitzer and her former husband Bob Leidy hosted a Christmas Eve party, where the highlight of the evening would be a visit from Santa. St. Nick—who bore more than a passing resemblance to the dashing Mr. Leidy—would appear on the roof and clamber down, to the delight of the thirty or more assembled children. Parents knew to bring a gift that would be placed in Santa's bag, which was pushed down the chimney so that every kid got an early present from Santa. "It started out for just our two boys," Liza says, "and it grew into this thing for two hundred people. We lived in fear that Bob would fall off the roof and land on the kids."

Santa Bob had a few years off, but with a new generation of kiddies—Bad Jack McCluskey and his cousin Kai Pulitzer—he's been pressed back into service. These days he walks, gasping, to the front door to greet the kids, saying his sled has broken down. The kids rescue him and drag him in the house and ply him with cigars, Coca-Cola™ and cookies, then get on with whispering in his ear. Last year the real Santa brought Jack a fish tank and, according to Dad, he hasn't turned on the TV once since.

Lilly's good friend Franci Dixon remembers a Christmas Eve long ago when she happened to mention she was serving Finnan Haddie—smoked haddock, a Scottish delicacy—the next morning for Christmas breakfast. "What?" exclaimed Peter Pulitzer. "We're coming." And on Christmas morning marching down the street came all five Pulitzers, barefoot in their bathrobes, pajamas and nightgowns.

"We'd tear through the gifts so we could get to Franci's," Lilly remembers. "She served these heavenly mad concoctions that zoomed us right through Christmas. Franci's Heavenlies."

These days, and in concert with lots of kids, Lilly's philosophy is simple: "I love to drag Christmas on for days." It makes sense, for that's when her son Peter and his family come out from California for a long visit. It's a rare time when her three kids, their spouses and her seven grandchildren can be together.

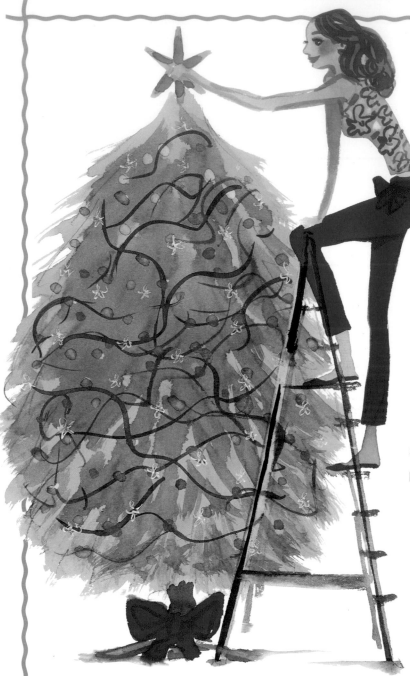

Needless to say, there's a lot of decorating. "Sometimes we have more fun decorating for Christmas than we do on Christmas itself," says Lilly. "We break out the garland and the tinsel and the lights and the balls and try to be organized about it, but it gets to be so silly and so much fun that half the stuff ends up on us before too long—and we're standing there covered in snowflakes and Christmas balls."

Among Lilly's treasured ornaments are a series of hand-painted porcelain balls that Franci Dixon—she of Finnan Haddie fame—created as a gift one year. Each one, personalized with a family member's name, spends eleven and a half months of the year carefully tucked away in a fabric-lined box, among the very special things Lilly calls "my treasures."

Some decorations are treasures, others are sheer inspiration: "I used to do upside-down Christmas trees, strung with lights, as chandeliers in the slat house. So pretty.

"Last year I bought this huge tree to put in the living room, the ceiling being very high. I changed my mind as we were lugging it in and chopped about six feet off the top! I ended up with this huge square tree with naturally no room for the star on top. I got all the lights on it and the tinsel, but ran out of steam when it came to putting on my few pathetic balls. I ended up putting everyone's Christmas card on the tree, and you know what? It looked great."

The Christmas Eve disease

"*Every Christmas,*" Lilly remembers, "we'd come down with a bad case of the 'Gozintas,' and even though it lasts less than twelve hours, it drove us batty. You know, the 'A goes into B, B goes into C' madness that comes when you're trying to assemble toys on Christmas Eve. The Gozintas!

"The happiest night of the year was when 'they' outgrew all that stuff!"

Christmas gifting

When it comes to buying presents, Lilly confesses, "I'm not a very good shopper. The moms tell me what the kids want—usually it's the biggie at the top of the list."

Amy Pulitzer, Peter's wife, remembers, "Lilly very seldom opens her gifts on Christmas Day. She likes to wait 'til the house quiets down, but sometimes it's three or four days later."

Christmas bests

Toy Store FAO Schwarz's revitalized Fifth Avenue store offers kids of all ages the most extraordinary toys, such as indoor tree houses to play in or a giant keyboard to play on. There are also concierge and personal shopping services to keep the big kids happy.

Movie *White Christmas* Great fun from Bing Crosby, Danny Kaye, Rosemary Clooney and Vera Ellen. Listen for Irving Berlin's songs, including the title classic. It's kind of silly and dopey, but doesn't that make it perfect?

Christmas in a foreign city London wins hands down for the Dickensian splendor that envelops the entire city at Christmas. Try to stay in one of the big old-fashioned hotels, like the Savoy or Claridges or the Connaught, and step back into the Edwardian era. There is also the Dorchester for some Art Deco panache.

Pageant Since 1933, Radio City Music Hall's Christmas Spectacular has been delighting audiences from all over the world. It features the Rockettes' famed *Parade of the Wooden Soldiers* as well as the living nativity scene. Its eight-week run is often sold out.

Lilly's favorite Christmas books

Lilly recommends these three for perfect Christmas reading.

The Joyous Season BY PATRICK DENNIS The man who brought us *Auntie Mame* returns with a hilarious and heartwarming saga of a brother and sister whose lives get upended when their parents split up on Christmas Day. "I read it and I could not stop laughing. It's that funny," recommends Lilly.

A Christmas Memory BY TRUMAN CAPOTE A happy and sad story based on Capote's childhood Christmases spent with an elderly cousin in a small town in Alabama. A modern classic.

'Twas The Night Before Christmas BY CLEMENT C. MOORE No household is complete without a copy of this second-most-famous of Christmas stories. It is a must-read on the night in question. If you visit Manhattan's New York Historical Society, you can see the desk and chair from where Moore composed his most famous work.

A CUBAN CHRISTMAS EVE DINNER

Roast pork leg with citrus marinade

Fresh pork leg is a huge cut of meat, and is an impressive centerpiece for a holiday feast. Lilly marinates the leg for a couple of days in a heady wine and fruit juice mixture with plenty of herbs and garlic. This roast is always cooked until very well done to dissolve all tough parts and to baste the meat from the inside out. Cubans would not serve gravy with this roast, being perfectly happy with its inherent juiciness, but Lilly bows to American custom with a light pan sauce. With a fifteen-pound roast, leftovers are more than likely and they will quickly disappear in sandwiches and other dishes. **12 OR MORE SERVINGS**

MARINADE

3 cups (and a splash more) dry white wine, such as Sauvignon Blanc

Grated zest of 2 oranges

1 cup fresh orange juice

Grated zest of 2 limes

½ cup fresh lime juice

6 scallions, white and green parts, chopped

12 garlic cloves, coarsely chopped

3 tablespoons dried oregano

2 tablespoons dried thyme

2 tablespoons dried rosemary

2 tablespoons salt

2 teaspoons crushed hot red pepper

1 fresh ham, also called pork leg, about 15 pounds

3 cups chicken broth

½ cup dry white wine, such as Sauvignon Blanc

1 tablespoon cornstarch

Salt and freshly ground pepper, to taste

At least 1 day before serving, make marinade: Combine wine, orange zest and juice, lime zest and juice, scallions, garlic, oregano, thyme, rosemary, salt and hot pepper in an extra-large roasting bag, such as one used for roast turkey.

Using a sharp knife, score pork skin in a crosshatch pattern, taking care not to go deeply into flesh. Place bagged marinade in a large roasting pan (this helps support and contain bag). Add pork to bag, and force out excess air. Tie bag closed. Refrigerate, turning pork occasionally in marinade, for at least 1 and up to 2 days.

Position rack in center of oven and preheat oven to 325°F. Remove bag from roasting pan and pork from marinade. Force some bits of garlic from marinade into the slits in skin. Discard marinade. Place pork on a roasting rack in roasting pan. Roast, occasionally basting with fat in pan (and removing excess fat in pan when it becomes more than a thin layer deep), until an instant-read thermometer inserted deep into center of roast reads 180°F, about 5½ hours. Transfer to a carving board and let stand for 20 to 30 minutes before carving.

Pour fat and juices in pan into a separating cup or glass bowl. Let stand 5 minutes. Pour (or skim) off fat; return pan juices back to pan. Heat pan over two burners on high heat until juices are sizzling. Add broth and bring to a boil, scraping up browned bits in pan. Dissolve cornstarch in ½ cup dry white wine, and then whisk into boiling broth and cook until thickened, about 5 minutes. Season with salt and pepper. Keep warm until ready to serve.

Using a carving knife, remove layer of crisp skin, but reserve for those who like it. Carve pork, with knife slightly diagonal to large bone. Pour sauce into sauceboat. Serve pork immediately, with sauce on the side.

Zucchini and grape tomatoes with cilantro

The exotic flavors in this menu need to be balanced by a light side dish. This sauté provides the equilibrium, and Christmas colors, as well. Have all of the ingredients ready before cooking, because this is a last-minute affair. 8 SERVINGS

4 tablespoons extra-virgin olive oil, divided

1 medium onion, chopped

2 garlic cloves, minced

4 medium zucchini (2 pounds), cut into ½-inch rounds

1 pint grape or cherry tomatoes, halved lengthwise

3 tablespoons chopped fresh cilantro

Salt and freshly ground pepper, to taste

Heat 2 tablespoons of oil in a large skillet over medium heat. Add onion and cook, stirring occasionally, until tender, about 4 minutes. Add garlic and cook until fragrant, about 1 minute. Transfer to a plate and wipe out skillet.

Heat remaining 2 tablespoons oil in skillet over medium-high heat. Add zucchini and cover. Cook, stirring occasionally, just until crisp-tender, about 6 minutes. Stir in tomatoes and onions. Cook, uncovered, just until tomatoes are heated through, about 2 minutes. Mix in cilantro and season with salt and pepper. Transfer to a serving dish and serve hot.

Yucca with mojo

This tuber, similar to potatoes, is beloved by Cubans, especially drizzled with mojo (mO-ho), a garlicky orange juice-based sauce. You can find yucca at Latino grocers and many supermarkets. Because it takes a bit of care to pare the yucca's tough skin and remove the core after cooking, Lilly (like many other cooks) usually works with frozen yucca. **12 SERVINGS**

4 pounds (about 4 medium) yucca (see Note)

MOJO

½ cup extra-virgin olive oil

3 garlic cloves, finely chopped

2 tablespoons fresh orange juice

2 tablespoons fresh lime juice

½ teaspoon salt

½ teaspoon freshly ground pepper

1 small white onion, thinly sliced, for garnish

Chopped cilantro or parsley, for garnish

Trim off narrow ends from each yucca. Cut yucca crosswise into 2- to 3-inch chunks. To pare, stand yucca on end on work surface. Using downward strokes, slice off tough skin. Quarter pared yucca lengthwise and transfer to a bowl of cold water. (Yucca can be prepared to this point 4 hours before cooking, and then stored at room temperature.) Drain and rinse yucca just before cooking.

Place yucca in a large soup pot and add cold, lightly salted water to cover. Bring to a boil over high heat. Reduce heat to medium and cook for 15 minutes. Add 1 cup of cold water to stop boiling, then return to a boil over high heat. (This cold water "shock" helps tenderize the tough yucca.) Reduce heat again and cook until yucca is barely tender when pierced with the tip of a knife, about 15 minutes more. Drain in a colander.

Meanwhile, make mojo. Heat oil and garlic in a small skillet over medium heat just until garlic begins to turn golden, about 3 minutes. Remove from heat. Add orange and lime juices, salt and pepper, and stir to dissolve salt. Set aside. (While best freshly made, mojo can be prepared up to 2 hours ahead, and then stored at room temperature.)

One chunk at a time, spear yucca with a fork. Remove any fibrous center core with another fork, and transfer yucca to a warm serving bowl. Drizzle with mojo. Garnish with onion and cilantro and serve.

NOTE: If you wish, substitute four 1½-pound bags frozen yucca for the fresh yucca. Frozen yucca has been pared and cored. Cook according to the package's instructions.

Black beans and rice

In Cuban kitchens, this side dish goes by many names. It can be called Moros y Christianos (Moors and Christians, for its black and white composition); when the beans and rice are cooked together, it's congee. No matter what it's called, it's hearty and tasty, especially with roast pork. **12 SERVINGS**

BLACK BEANS

½ cup diced salt pork (remove rind before dicing)

1 medium onion, chopped

½ cup diced (¼-inch) green bell pepper

2 garlic cloves, minced

1 large ripe tomato, halved, seeded and coarsely chopped

Four 15- to 19-ounce cans black beans, drained and rinsed

½ cup chicken broth

RICE

1½ cup long-grain rice

1½ cups chicken broth

½ teaspoon salt

To make beans, cook salt pork in a large saucepan over medium heat, stirring often, until it is browned and has rendered fat, about 7 minutes. Add onion, green pepper and garlic and cook, stirring often, until vegetables soften, about 5 minutes. Add tomatoes and cook, stirring often, until tomato is soft, about 5 minutes. Stir in black beans and broth. Cover and reduce heat to medium-low. Cook, stirring often, until beans are hot, about 20 minutes. (The beans can be prepared up to 2 days ahead, cooled, covered and refrigerated. Reheat gently over medium heat, adding a bit of broth, if needed, to keep beans from sticking to pot.)

Meanwhile, prepare rice. Combine rice, broth, 1½ cups water, and salt in a medium saucepan (liquid should come no higher than one-third up sides of pan; choose another pot, if necessary). Bring to a boil over high heat. Cover tightly and reduce heat to low. Simmer until rice is tender and has absorbed liquid, about 18 minutes. Remove from heat and let stand 5 minutes.

Stir rice into beans. Transfer to a serving bowl and serve hot.

Tres leches cake

While this cake is rumored to have been created in Nicaragua, cooks all over Latin America have appropriated it. The concept of soaking cake in liquid seems unlikely, but French cooks have been doing it for years, just not in a blend of three—regular, condensed and evaporated—milks. Usually served from a shallow pan, this layer cake version is a fancier (but not really more difficult) variation that turns tres leches into a gorgeous holiday dessert. 12 SERVINGS

CAKE

1 cup all-purpose flour

1 teaspoon baking powder

¼ teaspoon salt

⅓ cup milk

1 teaspoon vanilla

5 large eggs

¾ cup sugar

SOAKING MIXTURE

One 14-ounce can sweetened condensed milk

One 13-ounce can evaporated milk

½ cup whole milk

Whipped Cream (see page 135)

Assorted fresh fruit, such as pineapples, raspberries, kiwis and bananas, for serving

Position rack in center of oven and preheat to 350°F. Lightly butter inside of a 9-inch springform pan. Line bottom of pan with round of waxed paper. Flour inside of pan, tapping out excess flour.

For cake, sift flour, baking powder and salt onto a sheet of waxed paper. Mix milk and vanilla in a glass measuring cup. Place eggs in a bowl, cover with hot tap water and let stand for 5 minutes to warm eggs.

Crack eggs into the mixing bowl of a heavy-duty mixer; add sugar. Using whisk attachment on high speed, beat eggs until very pale and tripled in volume, about 5 minutes. (You can use a hand mixer, but it will take a few minutes longer to beat eggs.) Reduce speed to low. In thirds, beat in flour mixture, alternating with two equal additions of milk mixture, and blend just until smooth, scraping down sides of bowl as needed. Spread evenly in pan.

Bake until top of cake springs back when pressed in center and cake is barely pulling away from sides of pan, about 35 minutes. Cool on a wire cake rack for 10 minutes.

Run a knife around inside of pan to release cake, then remove sides of pan. Invert cake on a wire cake rack and remove bottom of pan. Pull off waxed paper. Wash, dry and reassemble springform pan. Return warm cake to pan, right side up. Pierce cake all over with a meat fork or wooden skewer.

For soaking mixture, whisk condensed, evaporated and whole milks until combined. Slowly pour soaking mixture over warm cake, stopping as needed to allow cake to absorb milk. Cover with plastic wrap and refrigerate until chilled, at least 4 hours or overnight. (The cake can be made up to 2 days ahead, and then covered and refrigerated.)

To serve, remove sides of springform pan. Place cake on pan bottom on a platter. Top cake with dollops of Whipped Cream and garnish with fresh fruit. Cut cake into wedges and serve chilled, with additional fruit.

Chicken hash on waffles

"My favorite Christmas breakfast…always…always…is chicken hash on waffles," says Lilly. The hash itself is a variation of the creamy chicken pot pie filling on page 133. Nothing beats freshly baked, homemade waffles, but Lilly believes you should have easy options ("Leggo my Eggo," says she). Bake homemade waffles ahead and freeze them to reheat before serving, or simply serve the hash on frozen waffles from the toaster. **8 TO 10 SERVINGS**

WAFFLES

1½ **cups all-purpose flour**

1 **tablespoon baking powder**

1 **tablespoon sugar**

¼ **teaspoon salt**

1½ **cups milk**

2 **large eggs**

6 **tablespoons (¾ stick) unsalted butter, melted**

Vegetable oil, for waffle iron

Chicken Hash (page 133)

Warm maple syrup, for serving

Unsalted butter, at room temperature, for serving

Position rack in center of oven and preheat oven to 200°F. Preheat a waffle iron according to manufacturer's instructions.

Sift flour, baking powder, sugar and salt into a medium bowl. Whisk milk, eggs and butter in another bowl. Pour into dry ingredients and whisk just until combined—a few lumps can remain. Wipe waffle iron grids with paper towel dipped in vegetable oil.

Ladle about ½ cup batter into center of heated waffle iron. Close lid and cook until waffles are golden brown, 3 to 5 minutes, depending on your iron. Transfer waffle directly to oven rack to keep warm while making remaining waffles. Do not place waffle on baking sheet—you want air to circulate around waffle. (The waffles can be made up to 2 weeks ahead, and then cooled completely, individually wrapped in plastic wrap and frozen. To reheat, unwrap frozen waffles and place directly on oven rack of preheated 350°F oven, and bake until heated through, about 5 minutes.) Makes about twenty 4-inch waffles.

For each serving, place one or two waffles on a warm plate, and top with chicken hash. Serve immediately, with warm maple syrup and soft butter.

Pomegranate and pineapple salad

Although pomegranates are becoming available practically year-round, they are traditionally harvested in winter. Their plump magenta seeds are filled with a tart, ambrosial juice that adds vibrant color and flavor to many dishes, such as this easy fruit salad. It does take a little knowledge to free the seeds without squirting the juice (it stains) all over you, but knowledge is power, and the instructions are below.

8 SERVINGS

1 pomegranate

1 ripe pineapple, pared, quartered, cored and cut into bite-size pieces

3 tablespoons fresh chopped mint

Fill a large bowl with cold water. Cutting skin through blossom end, score pomegranate into quarters, cutting no deeper than pale yellow pith. Immerse pomegranate in water and break pomegranate open at incisions. Still working under water, use fingers to release seeds from pith—seeds will sink to bottom of bowl. Pour off water with any bits of pith, then drain seeds.

Mix pomegranate seeds, pineapple and mint in a medium bowl. Cover and refrigerate until chilled, at least 1 and up to 8 hours. Serve chilled.

Raspberry sunrise mimosas

To make these attractive eye-openers, use a perfectly decent, but not expensive sparkling wine, and save the real champagne for another time. For extra elegance, serve in champagne flutes. ABOUT 6 DRINKS

¼ cup black raspberry liqueur, such as Chambord

2 cups fresh orange juice

One 750-mil bottle chilled sparkling wine or champagne

Thinly sliced orange rounds and mint sprigs, for garnish

For each drink, place a long spoon, such as an iced tea or bar spoon, in a glass. (This helps the sparkling wine or champagne from bubbling over when it hits the orange juice.) Add raspberry liqueur, then orange juice. Slowly pour in sparkling wine or champagne, taking care that it doesn't froth over. Garnish with orange slices and mint, and serve immediately.

NEW YEAR'S

"It was without a doubt the very best, most fun party in town. I think the reason being that you knew everyone in the room and we were all madly attractive!"

—LILLY, ON THE COCONUTS' NEW YEAR'S EVE BALL

On New Year's Eve the town of Palm Beach goes cuckoo for the Coconuts. And who or what exactly are the Coconuts? "The Coconuts are a group of bachelors who originally banded together years ago in the 1920s and threw a costume party on New Year's Eve to pay back all their invitations for the year," Lilly explains.

Single men were (and still are) a welcome addition to the Palm Beach social season and were (and still are) often invited out. Just as often, they lacked (and still do lack) either the means or the digs, or both, to return the invitations in kind. Just as there's safety in numbers, there's also thrift, hence the idea of throwing one big party, inviting everyone they owe and sharing the cost. And what better night than New Year's Eve for a spectacular blast?

What started with originally eight or nine bachelors has, over the years, grown in number. There are twenty-three Coconuts as of last count. Then—and now—it is the most sought-after invite in town. It is the place to be in Palm Beach at midnight.

Lilly fondly remembers the Coconuts parties as being "small, intimate and in the backroom of Ta-boó, with everyone squashed on the dance floor jigging their hearts out to the wonderful Cliff Hall and his boys. There were only a few tables to sit at so you just had to keep to the beat or sit on somebody's lap.

"I remember one New Year's Eve when, out of the corner of my eye, I saw this hairpiece go sailing by. A cat fight soon started and I think the hairless one got the point, which was not to dance quite so close!

"A breakfast of scrammies and sausages would be served giving us all our second and third winds.

"We'd conga up and down Worth Avenue, through Ta-boó and down to the Everglades, kissing everyone along the way," says Lilly.

The menus

NEW YEAR'S EVE DINNER

POTATO PANCAKES WITH CAVIAR AND SOUR CREAM

RACK OF LAMB WITH HERBED CRUST AND FRESH MINT SAUCE

RATATOUILLE WITH OLIVES

BUTTERY BABY SPINACH

MESCLUN WITH ORANGES, CUCUMBERS AND BALSAMIC-ORANGE VINAIGRETTE

FLOATING ISLANDS WITH ORANGE CUSTARD SAUCE

NEW YEAR'S DAY OPEN HOUSE

SMOKED SALMON PLATTER WITH DILLED SOUR CREAM

ANTIPASTO PLATTER

TORTELLINI AND BROCCOLI SALAD

DOUBLE CHOCOLATE BROWNIES

"Today that kind of New Year's Eve is either for the young or for someone more energized than me. I haven't been out in twenty years. Now on New Year's Eve I'm always home watching the ball drop."

Lilly may not be dancing all night these days, but she certainly rings in the New Year in a festive manner. "Every New Year's Eve when my brother Dinny and his wife Ande's kids were little they would come and stay with their favorite Aunt Lilly. Enrique would suit up and go with joy to the Coconuts. I would suit down and stay in my heavenly house with four of the greatest, funniest and most imaginative kids and Inga their nurse. I wouldn't swap those New Year's Eves for all the tea in you-know-where."

Now that the kids are grown up New Year's Eve might be a dinner party for close friends. It is one of the few seated dinners in her house, with the twin glass-topped tables in her dining room sparkling under the candlelight. Or there might be early evening cocktails, with just simple hors d'oeuvres and champagne to jump-start the night's revels.

This last idea evolved from a little party hiccup that Lilly experienced (and, yes, she's born a few hiccups in her day). She had prepared a big buffet for forty or fifty people only to discover that "no one wanted to eat. The kids just wanted to dress up, drink champagne and wait for the next party to start. Who at that age can be bothered with food?"

Not to worry, or to cry over uneaten chicken. "The next day," she says, "we threw the chicken in the oven with a couple of bottles of wine and some sauce from Costco and made a big casserole."

Smart idea, as casseroles frequently take center stage at the big buffet parties that Lilly loves to give—especially when it's something like a New Year's Day open house, where people will be drifting in and out all day long in various degrees of clearheadedness from the celebrations of the night before. Add a vast bowl of some kind of comfort food, a couple of side things that can just be picked at and some goodies for those with a sweet tooth, and you're set to go.

As the Christmas and New Year's holiday brings together the full clan, there are literally dozens of people—cousins, friends, aunts, uncles, neighbors and exes—in and out of the house, with the full variety of activities that the range of ages would suggest. Some people might be out for a game of tennis or golf, while the kids might be bouncing on the trampoline or playing Ping-Pong.

"When the tribe was all here New Year's week, I, as leader, decided we just had to have a group photo," Lilly says. "I called Katie Kuhner—that perfecto photographer—and told her to prepare herself and buy hundreds of rolls of film and get a good night's sleep. We gathered the next morning: me, Peter and his, Flo and hers, Liza and hers, Min and hers and my cousin M-m-maud (she stutters) and hers. At last count the group poolside was forty-four—every kid's kid plus exes, and even my niece Phoebe's manny (guy nanny). We just have to keep this up."

When friends tell Lilly, "It's so great that you have this open house," she responds, "Ha, I never think of it as ever being closed."

New Year's Eve plan B

If, like Lilly, you've got a lot of young people in your life and for them New Year's Eve means a multiple round of parties, follow her lead: keep some chilled champagne and a few savory treats on hand for your turn on the NYE rotation.

Your favorite bubbly will do nicely. As for hors d'oeuvres, "peanut butter and bacon has been done to death," Lilly gripes. "Let's come up with something new." Here are some alternatives that match Lilly's famous PB&B for both easy preparation and tastiness.

Pecans sautéed in butter, cajun seasoning, sugar and salt.

Celery stuffed with blended blue cheese and cream cheese, and then topped with walnuts.

Black and green olives (with pits), marinated in olive oil, grated lemon zest, lemon juice, red pepper flakes, garlic and rosemary.

A can of tuna tossed in the blender, along with some mayo, some capers and some lemon juice. Blend 'til smooth. Makes a great dip.

If you don't feel like doing the "full Balenciaga"

Here are two alternatives, albeit at opposite ends of the spectrum: snuggle in with your honey and a good DVD, or escape for a marvelous week of skiing.

The snuggle option:

The Poseidon Adventure It's New Year's Eve, the ship tips over and Shelley Winters goes all Esther Williams to rescue Gene Hackman. What could be better than that?

Bridget Jones's Diary It's Hugh Grant and Colin Firth fighting for Renée Zellweger's big heart.

When Harry Met Sally Billy Crystal takes Meg Ryan out for pastrami on rye…

The Apartment Jack Lemmon and Shirley MacLaine stay in and eat spaghetti strained on a tennis racquet.

About a Boy It's Hugh Grant (again). Can he find love at a New Year's Eve dinner party? Too much Hugh? Never.

Allons pour faire du ski, or Go Glam

While there's always Vail, Aspen and even the snowboard-free Deer Valley in Utah, why not indulge yourself and jet off to Les Trois Vallées region of France. The towns of Val d'Isère, Courchevel and Méribel offer some of the most spectacular skiing in the world, along with some of the best restaurants and dining experiences. Go on, you deserve the best, non?

Resolute resolutions for any New Year

Absolutely NO whining.

Take good care of those you love.

Read at least one book a month.

Try to remember people's names.

Don't be "special"! (Don't cause a fuss, never be a bother and always mind your manners!)

Potato pancakes with caviar and sour cream

These crispy potato pancakes topped with caviar are a classic example of plain and fancy. Have everything at the ready (peeled potatoes in water, sour cream at room temperature) to make the pancakes at the last minute; they're at their best when served right from the skillet. And don't skimp on the oil to fry pancakes, or they won't get properly crunchy. Lilly is a big fan of American paddlefish caviar, which is every bit as good, but much less expensive, as the imported variety.

8 SERVINGS

1½ **pounds baking potatoes, peeled**

1 **medium onion, peeled**

2 **large eggs, beaten**

2 **tablespoons dried bread crumbs**

1 **teaspoon salt**

½ **teaspoon freshly ground pepper**

Vegetable oil for frying

¾ **cup sour cream, at room temperature**

2 **ounces caviar, preferably paddlefish**

Chopped fresh chives, for garnish

Grate potatoes in a food processor fitted with a large shredding blade (or use the large holes of a box grater). Grate onion into potatoes. A handful at a time, working over sink, squeeze excess moisture from potato-onion mixture, and place squeezed vegetables into a medium bowl. Add eggs, bread crumbs, salt and pepper, and mix well.

Place two large skillets over medium-high heat. Add enough oil to each skillet to come ⅛ inch up the sides and heat until oil is shimmering. Measure about ⅓ cup batter and transfer in measuring cup to skillets. Spread out batter with back of cup to make eight 4-inch-diameter pancakes. Cook until the undersides are golden brown, 2 to 3 minutes. Turn and cook to crisp the other sides, about 2 minutes more. Transfer to paper towels.

To serve, place each pancake on a salad plate. Top each with a dollop of sour cream and equal amounts of caviar. Sprinkle with chives and serve immediately.

Rack of lamb with herbed crust and fresh mint sauce

Here are two terrific reasons why rack of lamb is a great entrée for a special dinner party. First, it can be prepared an hour or so ahead of the final roasting. Equally important, it is as sophisticated as it is delicious. This recipe assumes that you will be using Australian or New Zealand lamb, which is smaller than the American variety and is what most butchers are carrying now at the best price. Four chops per serving may seem like a lot, but the actual amount of meat can be small, so it's best to roast four racks as not to be caught short. The fresh Mint Sauce is light and lively. **8 SERVINGS**

Four 8-rib racks of lamb, about 1½ pounds each, trimmed of excess fat, bones Frenched (that is, scraped clean)

1 teaspoon salt

½ teaspoon pepper

½ cup Dijon mustard

2 tablespoons herbes de Provençe

2 garlic cloves, crushed through a press

2 cups fresh bread crumbs (made from crusty day-old bread in a food processor or blender)

Mint Sauce (recipe follows)

Position rack in center of oven and preheat oven to 450°F. Lightly oil a large rimmed baking sheet.

Heat a large empty skillet over medium-high heat. Season lamb with salt and pepper. Working in batches, place rack of lamb in skillet, fat side down. Cook until underside is browned, about 3 minutes. Using tongs to hold lamb steady, sear top edge and sides of rack, taking about 2 more minutes. Pour out fat in skillet as it accumulates.

Mix mustard, herbs and garlic in a small bowl. Using the back of a spoon, spread mustard mixture over meaty top and curved edge of each rack. Spread bread crumbs in a shallow dish. Coat mustard-coated surface of each rack with crumbs, pressing them to adhere. To fit four racks on one baking sheet, interlace ribs of two racks, crumbed-sides facing out, and stand them together on the sheet. Repeat with other two racks. (The lamb can be prepared 1½ hours ahead, and then stored at cool room temperature.)

Bake until crust is tipped with brown and a meat thermometer inserted in center of rack reads 130°F for medium-rare meat, about 20 minutes. (Because racks are small, it may be easiest to insert thermometer horizontally through the eye of the meat to reach the center.) Transfer racks to a cutting board. Tent racks with foil and let stand for 5 minutes.

Cut each rack into 8 chops and arrange chops on a platter. Serve with Mint Sauce passed on the side.

MINT SAUCE: Dissolve 2 tablespoons sugar in ½ cup boiling water in a small bowl. Add 1 cup chopped fresh mint leaves and let cool. Stir in 2 tablespoons white wine vinegar. Pour into a sauceboat and serve within 1 hour of making.

Ratatouille with olives

Ratatouille, the Provençal vegetable ragout, is so perfect with rack of lamb that it is a wasted effort to try and come up with something that is better. The olives also add a certain flair. Be careful not to overcook. Ratatouille is so much better when each vegetable retains its own character. 8 SERVINGS

1 eggplant (about 1⅓ pounds), cut into 1-inch chunks

1 teaspoon salt, plus more to taste

¾ cup extra-virgin olive oil, divided

1 medium onion, chopped

1 red bell pepper, seeded and chopped

4 garlic cloves, finely chopped

One 15-ounce can diced tomatoes in juice

1 tablespoon herbes de Provençe

¼ teaspoon crushed hot red pepper, plus more to taste

2 large zucchini, quartered lengthwise, then cut crosswise into ½-inch-thick pieces

½ cup pitted and coarsely chopped black Mediterranean olives, such as kalamata

Toss eggplant with salt in a large colander. Let stand to drain off juices, about 1 hour. Rinse under cold water and pat dry with paper towels.

Meanwhile, about 15 minutes before eggplant has finished draining, heat 2 tablespoons of oil in a large heavy saucepan, preferably enameled cast iron, over medium heat. Add onion, red bell pepper and garlic. Cook, stirring often, until vegetables soften, about 5 minutes. Add tomatoes with juice, herbs and crushed hot pepper, and bring to a boil.

Heat 2 tablespoons of oil in a large skillet over medium-high heat. Add zucchini and cook, stirring often, just until crisp-tender, about 6 minutes. Add to tomato sauce and mix well. Remove from heat until ready to add eggplant.

Heat remaining ½ cup oil in a large skillet over medium-high heat until oil is very hot and shimmering. Add eggplant and cook, stirring occasionally, until lightly browned and tender, about 10 minutes. Although eggplant may soak up oil, do not add more oil to skillet unless absolutely necessary to avoid burning. Transfer eggplant to tomato sauce.

Bring ratatouille to a boil over high heat, stirring occasionally. Reduce heat to low and cover. Simmer, stirring occasionally, to blend the flavors, about 10 minutes. During the last 5 minutes, stir in olives. (The ratatouille can be prepared 3 days ahead, and then cooled, covered and refrigerated. Reheat over medium heat.) Season with salt and crushed hot pepper. Transfer to a serving dish and serve hot.

Buttery baby spinach

Super-efficient baby spinach, washed, stemmed and ready to cook, can be found in bags at every super-market. It can soak up a lot of butter, which gives it an irresistible flavor. 8 SERVINGS

4 tablespoons (½ stick) unsalted butter, divided

3 tablespoons chopped shallots

1 garlic clove, minced

2 pounds baby spinach

Salt and freshly ground pepper, to taste

Melt 2 tablespoons of butter in a large saucepan over medium heat. Add shallots and garlic and cook until shallots soften, about 2 minutes. Add half of the spinach and cover. Cook, stirring often, until spinach wilts, about 3 minutes.

Stir in remaining spinach and 2 tablespoons butter. Cover and cook, stirring often, until spinach is tender, about 5 minutes. Season with salt and pepper. Using a slotted spoon, transfer to a serving dish and serve hot.

Mesclun with oranges, cucumbers and balsamic-orange vinaigrette

Look for some of the more exotic varieties of oranges, such as magenta-fleshed blood oranges or the sweet Temples. Here, they add color and tang to green salad, accented with the crunch of English cucumber.
8 SERVINGS

4 oranges, such as blood or Temple

3 tablespoons balsamic vinegar

1½ tablespoons finely chopped shallots

¾ cup extra-virgin olive oil

Salt and freshly ground pepper, to taste

1 seedless (English) cucumber, thinly sliced

12 ounces mesclun (mixed spring greens), rinsed and dried

Grate zest from 1 orange and set aside. Using a serrated knife, cut top and bottom of 1 orange so the orange will stand on work surface. Cut with downward strokes to remove orange skin where it meets flesh. Working over a bowl, cut between membranes to release orange segments, letting segments fall into bowl. Cover and refrigerate until ready to serve.

Holding orange segments, drain orange juice from bowl into a small bowl. Add orange zest, vinegar and shallots, and whisk to combine. Gradually whisk in oil. Season with salt and pepper. (The vinaigrette can be prepared 1 day ahead, and then covered and refrigerated. Whisk well to recombine.)

Toss orange segments and cucumber slices with 2 table-spoons vinaigrette in a medium bowl. Toss mesclun with remaining vinaigrette in a large bowl. Divide equal amounts of greens among 8 plates, and top with oranges and cucumber. Serve chilled.

Floating Islands with orange custard sauce

"If there's one thing I want to have in this book," says Lilly, "it's a recipe for Îles Flotantes. My favorite dessert of all time." A standard on French bistro menus, Lilly and her sister Flo remember savoring their own bowls of Floating Islands topped with a big spoonful of currant jelly. The ethereal meringue "islands" floating in a custard sea make the dessert seem light, when in fact the luscious sauce is far from diet fare. But who cares? Because the meringues are egg-shaped, Lilly calls these Oeufs à l'Orange, or "orange eggs." **8 SERVINGS**

MERINGUES

¼ **cup fresh lemon juice**

8 **large egg whites (save the yolks for the sauce)**

¼ **teaspoon cream of tartar**

1 **cup sugar**

ORANGE CUSTARD SAUCE

3 **cups half-and-half**

4 **wide strips orange zest (use a vegetable peeler)**

9 **large egg yolks (8 from the meringue white plus 1 extra)**

¾ **cup sugar**

2 **tablespoons orange-flavored liqueur, such as Grand Marnier**

1 **teaspoon vanilla extract**

Red currant jelly, for serving

Thin strips of orange zest (use a citrus zester), for garnish

To make meringues, bring 4 quarts water and lemon juice to a bare simmer in a large saucepan over medium heat. Reduce heat to low. Line a large baking sheet with a clean, lint-free kitchen towel.

Beat whites in a very clean large bowl with an electric mixer on low until whites are foamy. Add cream of tartar and increase speed to high. Beat just until whites form soft peaks; do not overbeat. One tablespoon at a time, beat in sugar and beat until whites are stiff and shiny, but not dry.

Working over the saucepan of barely simmering water, use two large soup spoons to shape meringue into 4 egg-shaped mounds (or as close to an egg shape as you can come without being a professional French pastry chef), dropping them gently into water. Do not crowd meringues; they will expand. Cover and poach meringues until undersides are set, about 2 minutes. It is very important that water does not go beyond a bare simmer, or meringues will deflate. Using a slotted spoon, turn meringues gently, cover and poach other sides. Use slotted spoon to transfer meringues to towel. Continue to make a total of 16 meringues. (The meringues can be prepared 1 day ahead, and then cooled, covered with plastic wrap and refrigerated.)

To make sauce, heat half-and-half and orange zest in a heavy-bottomed medium saucepan over medium heat until simmering. Whisk egg yolks and sugar in a medium bowl until very pale and thick. Gradually whisk in half of hot cream mixture. Pour into saucepan. Cook over low heat, stirring constantly with a wooden spoon, until sauce coats spoon (a finger run down the spoon will leave a path in sauce) and an instant-read thermometer reads 185°F, about 3 minutes. Strain through a wire sieve into a medium bowl; discard zest. Cool completely. Stir in liqueur and vanilla. Cover and refrigerate until chilled, at least 2 hours. (The sauce can be prepared up to 1 day ahead, and then cooled, covered and refrigerated.)

To serve, pour equal amounts of chilled sauce into 8 shallow bowls. Top each with 2 meringues. Top with a spoonful of red currant jelly, and garnish with orange zest. Serve chilled.

Smoked salmon platter with dilled sour cream

Even if your New Year's open house buffet starts in the early afternoon, there will be some guests who have had a late night, and your meal will be their first repast of the day. This breakfasty-brunchy spread is for them. Look for vacuum-packed smoked salmon at your price club, or order it well ahead of the party from your local delicatessen (as they will undoubtedly be very busy during the New Year's holiday).

12 SERVINGS

DILLED SOUR CREAM

1 pint sour cream

$\frac{1}{3}$ cup chopped fresh dill

$\frac{1}{2}$ teaspoon freshly ground pepper

$1\frac{1}{2}$ pounds thinly sliced smoked salmon

Thinly sliced onion, lemon wedges, capers and salmon caviar, for serving

Mini-bagels or sliced baguette, for serving

To make dilled sour cream, mix sour cream, dill and pepper in a small bowl. Transfer to a serving bowl and cover. Refrigerate for at least 1 hour or overnight.

Arrange smoked salmon on a serving platter. Place onion, lemon, capers and caviar in separate bowls. Serve with mini-bagels or sliced baguette.

Antipasto platter

The Italians have a word for a sumptuous spread of food: "abbodanza." That's the word to keep in mind when designing an antipasto platter for a party. It should be abundant and overflowing with lots of good things to eat. Pay a visit to the best Italian deli in town and stop short of buying the place out. Here are some suggestions just to get you started.

12 SERVINGS

Sliced Prosciutto di Parma

Sliced salami, sopressata and coppa

Black or green Mediterranean olives

Marinated mushrooms, artichokes and red and yellow peppers

Grilled eggplant and zucchini with balsamic vinaigrette

Roasted artichoke spread or olivada (black olive paste)

Ripe melon and clusters of grapes

Fresh mozzarella and chunks of Parmigiano Reggiano

Bread sticks and foccacia

Tortellini and broccoli salad

This tasty salad, with a hint of garlic and oregano, is as substantial as it is colorful. Broccoli is usually pretty good in winter, and makes a fine salad. If you'd like to bulk it up a bit more, add some chopped salami or ham. 10 TO 12 SERVINGS

1 large head broccoli

2 pounds frozen cheese tortellini, preferably tricolor

3 tablespoons red wine vinegar

1 teaspoon dried oregano

1 garlic clove, crushed through a press

1 teaspoon salt, plus more to taste

$\frac{1}{4}$ teaspoon crushed hot red pepper flakes

$\frac{3}{4}$ cup extra-virgin olive oil

One 12-ounce jar roasted red peppers, drained and chopped

1 cup pitted and chopped kalamata olives

4 scallions, white and green parts, chopped

$\frac{1}{4}$ cup chopped parsley

Bring a soup pot of lightly salted water to a boil over high heat. (You need a big pot to cook the tortellini.) Cut broccoli into florets, reserving stems. Peel stems, and cut crosswise into ¼-inch-thick rounds.

Add stems to water and cook 3 minutes. Add florets and cook until broccoli is just crisp-tender, about 3 minutes more. Using a skimmer or wire sieve, transfer broccoli to a bowl of cold water, keeping water boiling. Drain broccoli and pat dry with paper towels.

Add tortellini to water and cook according to package instructions until tender. Drain, rinse under cold water and drain again well.

Whisk vinegar, oregano, garlic, salt and crushed red pepper flakes in a large bowl. Gradually whisk in oil. Add tortellini, broccoli, chopped red peppers, olives, scallions and parsley. Mix well. (The salad can be made 8 hours ahead, and then covered and refrigerated.) Serve chilled or at room temperature.

Double chocolate brownies

Fans of thick, ultra-chocolately brownies STOP and look no further. As if these weren't rich enough, they include chocolate chips in the batter and a thin layer of chocolate icing, too. After all, come January 2 the diets begin, so we may as well go out with a bang. While you could buy brownies at a bakery, nothing beats the homemade version. These couldn't be easier, and you'll get a big batch for your minimal efforts. Cut them bite-size, and you'll have quite a stack.

16 LARGE BROWNIES

1 cup (2 sticks) unsalted butter, cut up, plus softened butter for the pan

11 ounces bittersweet or semisweet chocolate

1 cup packed light brown sugar

¾ cup granulated sugar

¼ cup light corn syrup or honey

4 large eggs, at room temperature

2 teaspoons vanilla extract

2½ cups all-purpose flour, plus more for the pan

½ teaspoon baking soda

½ teaspoon salt

2 cups (12 ounces) semisweet chocolate chips, divided

Position rack in center of oven and preheat to 350°F. Lightly butter a 13 X 9-inch metal baking pan. Line bottom and two short sides of pan with 18-inch length of aluminum foil (preferably nonstick foil), pleating the foil lengthwise to make a 9-inch-wide strip. Fold foil hanging over two short ends to make "handles." Dust exposed areas of pan with flour and tap out excess.

Melt butter in a large saucepan over medium heat. Remove from heat and stir in chopped chocolate. Let stand until chocolate softens, about 3 minutes, then whisk until smooth. Whisk in brown and granulated sugars and corn syrup or honey. One at a time, whisk in eggs, then vanilla.

Sift flour, baking soda and salt together. Add to chocolate mixture and stir in pan until smooth. Mix in half of chocolate chips. Spread evenly in pan.

Bake just until a toothpick inserted in center of brownie comes out with a moist crumb, 40 to 45 minutes. Do not overbake. Place pan on a wire cake rack. Sprinkle with remaining 1 cup chips. Let stand until chips are shiny, about 5 minutes. Using a metal spatula, spread melted chips into thin layer over brownie. Cool completely.

Run a knife between brownie and unlined pan sides to release brownie. Lift up on foil handles to remove brownie in one piece. Peel off and discard foil. Cut brownie into 16 pieces. If you wish, cut brownies into bite-size pieces for more servings. (The brownies can be made up to 2 days ahead, and then individually wrapped in plastic wrap and stored at room temperature.)

VALENTINE'S DAY

✽

"Roses are red,
Violets are green,
Just leave me at home,
So I won't have to scream!"

—LILLY

To Lilly Valentine's Day is not about romance, soft music, cupcakes shaped like hearts and dinner for two in some overpriced crowded restaurant. "No sireee, Bob," she exclaims. "My favorite VD would start the week before, picking out Valentines for the loves in my life. The loves, I might add, having nothing to do with what you might think. My loves range from age four to fifty and they're really splendid—each and every one of them. I hit the bank, stuff the little darlings with crisp greens and hit the Post Office. How easy is that? I love it. They love it and I don't have to have a violin in my ear for two hours.

"Hot-spit!," adds Lilly. "Having got all that off my chest, what shall we do for Valentine's Day?"

What to do for Valentine's Day, indeed? True, the original Saint Valentine, martyred for disobeying Emperor Claudius' ban on conducting marriages in third-century Rome, had it rough. But it's just as tough today. Either you don't have that special someone so Valentine's Day red turns into the blues real fast, or you do have that special someone and Valentine's Day puts you quite literally in the red with the cost of that romantic dinner for two and the dozen roses.

One way to become a hero to your friends—attached and not—is to do something that leaves the romance in and keeps the stress out. "How about a little Hearts-and-Posies Supper Dance for lovebirds?" suggests Lilly with just a tad of mischievous irony in her voice. "I love piano music and all the great romantic songs. Combine those with a little supper and a lot of red and we're set to go."

A supper dance

GRILLED BEEF TENDERLOIN WITH WILD
MUSHROOM SAUCE

BABY CARROTS WITH MADEIRA GLAZE

SCALLOPED POTATOES WITH CELERY
ROOT AND GRUYÈRE

ENDIVE, APPLE AND ROQUEFORT SALAD
WITH WALNUT VINAIGRETTE

WHITE CHOCOLATE CHEESECAKE WITH
PASSION FRUIT SAUCE

Supper clubs, like the Rainbow Room, the Stork Club, El Morocco and the Blue Angel, were a staple of the New York social scene when Lilly came out as a debutante in the late 1940s. Formal dress was required, with a cover charge in the $1.50 to $2.00 range. Each club offered an intimate atmosphere, good food and a small orchestra for dancing. You could either make a night of it, or drop in after dinner or the theater.

"When I was seventeen and eighteen, Fred, my bestest friend, would drive down from Yale every Thursday night," Lilly remembers. "We would have dinner at Mother's apartment at the Westbury (noth-

ing like starting off with room service) and then hit every piano bar in town. We would just have to hear Ralph Strain, Goldie Hawkins, Cy Waters and, of course, Hugh Shannon. We did this every Thursday for quite some time. There was nothing like it. Freddie would then jump in his car and head back to New Haven. We just loved our Thursdays.

"I used to go to La Rue and the Stork Club and El Morocco. In fact, the inspiration for the Club CacaLoco birthday party we threw for Enrique was 'El-Mos', which was famous for its zebra-patterned upholstered banquettes. Enrique went there all the time in the old days."

An old-fashioned supper dance, with everyone getting just a little dressed up, a menu that's just a tad bit more extravagant than normal and a piano player to fill the room with favorite songs to both dance and sing along to is sure to capture the imaginations and, maybe, the hearts of your friends. Who knows? You might end up giving Cupid a run for his money?

Ask everyone to wear red in one shade or another, from pale pink to deepest burgundy. Fill the room with red and pink balloons on shimmering silver streamers. String a variety of Valentine's Day cards—some romantic, some naughty, some silly, some fun—around the room and have different people read them aloud.

Start the dancing as people walk through the door, so there's an air of festivity right off the bat. Tell everyone to watch old Fred Astaire movies for inspiration. (You may have to remind some that the phrase, "Let's face the music and dance," is an invitation, not a death sentence.) Have them bring a list of requested songs so that everyone can hear their favorite.

There are a hundred ways you can make the evening memorable. Just remember to keep it fun, keep it light and, Lilly advises, "Don't make it sappy. Give it some zip, some zest and who knows how many more Valentines you'll have next year!"

Nobody does it better: a Fred and Ginger primer

Fred Astaire and Ginger Rogers were the best dance partners in the history of Hollywood, and maybe just about everyplace else. They danced to music written by the crème de la crème of American composers—Cole Porter, Irving Berlin, Jerome Kern and so on. Here they are at their most sublime:

Follow the Fleet When they "Face the Music and Dance."

Roberta They both say, "I won't dance," but they do.

Shall We Dance? Indeed, they shall.

Swing Time They claim they're "Never Gonna Dance," but one should never say never.

Top Hat They (and we) are in heaven when they're dancing "Cheek to Cheek"!

Our favorite romantic music

If you know no chanteuse to bring in for your dance, don't fret. Grab a couple of these CDs for an acceptable substitute.

A Wonderful World Tony Bennett and k.d. lang. Since their first pairing on an MTV Unplugged special, this musical odd couple has perfected a heavenly partnership.

The Dana Owens Album Queen Latifah moves beyond hip-hop to the smoky rooms of jazz and R&B, doing so with grace and style.

Simply Streisand Barbra doing what she does best: simply singing great songs, among them possibly the most romantic song of all time, Jerome Kern's "All the Things You Are."

Ella Fitzgerald Sings the Cole Porter Songbook The queen of jazz and the king of popular Tin Pan Alley songs meet and sparks fly.

Songs for Young Lovers One of Sinatra's very best, topping even his *Songs for Swingin' Lovers*.

Our favorite cards

For the best in disarmingly risqué Valentine's Day cards, go to Vivi's on the Via Parigi in Palm Beach and ask Tim to see his "under the counter" collection. Tell him Lilly sent you. And always remember Lilly's rule: never sign a Valentine.

Just the two of you...

Consider a quiet getaway to one side of the pond or the other, at two hotels where luxury is omnipresent but never taken for granted.

Mandarin Oriental Hotel, New York Towering above Central Park in the new Time Warner building, where you'll find champagne and caviar waiting in your room, a breathtaking sky spa and two of the finest restaurants in the city, the hotel's Asiate and, downstairs in the new Time Warner building, Gray Kunz's Café Gray.

Scotsman Hotel, Edinburgh For the serious luxury maven, the Scotsman, located in one of Europe's most romantic, and yet undiscovered, cities is the place for two. 120 roses and dinner cooked by your personal chef are just two of the highlights of a romantic Valentine's Day trip.

Grilled beef tenderloin with wild mushroom sauce

Beef tenderloin is an extravagance, but there is very little waste and its buttery texture is hard to surpass. Beef broth plays a big role in the success of the sauce, so try to use homemade (some butchers and gourmet shops have good frozen beef stock) or take Lilly's suggestion for gussying up canned broth.

8 TO 10 SERVINGS

MARINADE

1 cup hearty red wine, such as Zinfandel

¼ cup extra-virgin olive oil

4 garlic cloves, smashed

1 tablespoon Dijon mustard

1 tablespoon herbes de Provençe

1 teaspoon salt

½ teaspoon freshly ground pepper

1 beef tenderloin, trimmed and tied (about 3½ pounds)

WILD MUSHROOM SAUCE

7 tablespoons (½ stick plus 3 tablespoons) unsalted butter, divided

½ cup minced shallots

¼ cup all-purpose flour

2 cups beef broth, preferably homemade (see Note)

1 cup hearty red wine, such as Zinfandel

⅛ teaspoon dried thyme

1 pound cremini mushrooms, thinly sliced

Salt and freshly ground pepper, to taste

To make marinade, whisk together red wine, olive oil, garlic, mustard, herbs, salt and pepper. Place beef in a large zippered plastic bag and pour marinade over meat. Seal and refrigerate for at least 2 and up to 8 hours, occasionally turning bag. Remove from refrigerator 1 hour before grilling.

Meanwhile, while beef marinates, make mushroom sauce. Melt 2 tablespoons of butter in a medium saucepan over medium heat. Add shallots and cook, stirring occasionally, until lightly browned, about 4 minutes. Add 2 more tablespoons butter to saucepan and melt. Whisk in flour. Reduce heat to medium-low and let roux bubble without browning for 2 minutes. Stir in broth, wine and thyme and bring to a boil over medium heat. Cook uncovered, whisking occasionally, until sauce is lightly thickened and reduced by about one-quarter, about 20 minutes.

Melt 2 tablespoons butter in a large skillet over medium-high heat. Add mushrooms, and cook, stirring occasionally, until mushrooms are browned, 10 minutes. Add sauce and bring to a boil, scraping up browned bits in skillet. Season with salt and pepper. Dot top with remaining 1 tablespoon butter to keep a skin from forming. (The sauce can be stored at room temperature for 2 hours. Or cool, cover and refrigerate sauce for up to 1 day. Reheat over low heat.)

Build a charcoal fire on one side of an outdoor grill and let it burn until the coals are covered with white ash. Or, in a gas grill, preheat on high; then turn one burner off, leaving the other burner(s) on high. Lightly oil the cooking rack.

Remove beef from marinade and pat dry with paper towels. Place tenderloin over coals and cover. Grill, turning occasionally, until seared on all sides, about 10 minutes. Move beef to empty side of grill. In gas grill, grill beef over high burner, covered, turning occasionally, until seared on all sides, about 10 minutes. Move beef to off burner.

Continue grilling, covered, until an instant-read thermometer inserted in center of beef reads 130°F for medium-rare, about 20 minutes. Check meat temperature often to avoid overcooking.

Let beef stand for 10 minutes before removing twine. Carve crosswise into ½-inch-thick slices and serve with mushroom sauce.

NOTE: If you don't have homemade beef broth, you can easily embellish canned broth. Brown 1 beef shank (about 12 ounces) in 1 tablespoon vegetable oil in a medium saucepan over medium-high heat, about 8 minutes; transfer to a plate. Add 1 small chopped onion and 1 small chopped carrot to fat in saucepan and cook until browned, about 6 minutes. Return beef to saucepan. Add one 13½-ounce can beef broth and 3 cups water. Bring to a boil over high heat, skimming off foam that rises to surface. Reduce heat to low and add ⅛ teaspoon dried thyme. Partially cover and simmer for 1½ to 2 hours. Strain (the beef can be eaten), let stand 5 minutes, then skim fat off surface. Makes about 4 cups beef broth.

Baby carrots with Madeira glaze

Every household should have a solid recipe for glazed carrots, as they go so well with many roasts. Lilly insists on true baby carrots, available at the best grocers and produce shops, and not the taste-free baby-cut carrots that are merely carved from big carrots. Madeira is a Portuguese fortified wine, similar to sherry, which can act as a substitute, if you wish.

8 SERVINGS

2 pounds baby carrots, peeled and greens trimmed

3 tablespoons unsalted butter

¼ cup packed brown sugar

¼ cup Madeira

Salt and freshly ground pepper, to taste

Bring a large pot of lightly salted water to a boil over high heat. Add carrots and cook just until tender, about 5 minutes. Drain, rinse under cold running water, and drain again. Pat dry with paper towels. (The carrots can be prepared up to 1 day ahead, and then wrapped in fresh towels, stored in plastic bags and refrigerated.)

Melt butter in a large skillet over medium heat. Add brown sugar and Madeira and whisk until smooth. Add carrots and cover. Cook, stirring often, until carrots are heated through and glazed, about 3 minutes. Transfer to a serving dish, and season with salt and pepper to taste. Serve hot.

Scalloped potatoes with celery root and Gruyère

This recipe is so delicious that it will probably become your favorite for scalloped potatoes. A food processor makes quick work of slicing the potatoes and celery root, but you can use a knife. **8 SERVINGS**

2 tablespoons unsalted butter, softened

3 cups heavy cream

12 garlic cloves, crushed under a knife and peeled

2 pounds baking potatoes (russet), peeled

2 pounds celery root (celariac), pared and cut into quarters, with soft core trimmed out

1½ teaspoons salt

½ teaspoon freshly ground pepper

1 cup (4 ounces) shredded Gruyère cheese

Position rack in center of oven and preheat oven to 400°F. Generously coat inside of a 9 X 13-inch glass, ceramic or enameled cast iron baking dish with the butter.

Bring cream and garlic to a simmer in a medium saucepan over medium heat. Using a food processor fitted with a slicing blade, cut potatoes and celery root into ⅛-inch-thick slices. Spread half of potatoes and celery root into baking dish. Season with half of salt and pepper, and sprinkle with Gruyère. Using a slotted spoon, remove garlic from cream and scatter over Gruyère. Top with remaining potatoes and celery root. Pour cream over all. Press potatoes and celery root down to level them, barely covering in cream. Season with remaining salt and pepper. Cover tightly with aluminum foil.

Bake for 1 hour. Uncover and bake until potatoes and celery root are tender and top is golden brown, about 20 minutes. (The scalloped potatoes and celery root can be prepared up to 8 hours ahead, and then cooled, covered and kept at room temperature. Reheat, loosely covered with foil, in preheated 350°F oven, about 25 minutes.) Let stand 10 minutes. Serve hot.

Endive, apple and Roquefort salad with walnut vinaigrette

If your Valentine's Day party is a seated dinner, use this crisp salad as a first course. It also goes well with the rest of the menu if you're having a buffet. If you can't find the spear-shaped red endive or radicchio de Treviso, round radicchio is perfectly fine. **8 SERVINGS**

WALNUT VINAIGRETTE

¾ **cup vegetable oil**

½ **cup chopped walnuts**

3 **tablespoons white wine vinegar**

Salt and freshly ground pepper, to taste

1 **large head Boston lettuce, torn into bite-size pieces**

2 **heads Belgian endive, separated into leaves**

1 **head red endive or radicchio de Treviso, separated into leaves, or 1 head round radicchio, torn into bite-size pieces**

2 **Granny Smith apples, cored and thinly sliced**

1 **cup (about 5 ounces) Roquefort cheese, crumbled**

To make vinaigrette, combine oil and walnuts in an electric blender and blend until walnuts are very finely chopped. Pour into a glass measuring cup. Add vinegar to blender. With machine running, add walnut oil in a steady stream. Season with salt and pepper. (The vinaigrette can be made up to 1 day ahead, and then covered and refrigerated. Let come to room temperature and whisk to combine.)

Mix lettuce, endive, red endive or radicchio and apples in a large salad bowl. Add vinaigrette and toss well. Sprinkle with the Roquefort and serve immediately.

White chocolate cheesecake with passion fruit sauce

There is cheesecake, and then there is this outra-geously creamy, utterly seductive cheesecake. The secret ingredient is white chocolate (both chocolate and vanilla are considered aphrodisiacs by some). White chocolate is quick to scorch, so it should never be melted over direct heat. To gild the lily, garnish the cheesecake with heart-shaped cookies. 12 SERVINGS

CRUST

1 cup vanilla wafer crumbs (about 25 cookies, crushed in a food processor or blender)

2 tablespoons unsalted butter, melted

2 tablespoons sugar

FILLING

½ cup heavy cream

9 ounces high-quality white chocolate, finely chopped

Three 8-ounce packages cream cheese, well softened at room temperature (remove from refrigerator at least 2 hours before using)

4 large eggs, beaten

½ cup plus 2 tablespoons sugar

1½ teaspoons vanilla extract

GLAZE

2 tablespoons heavy cream

2 ounces high-quality white chocolate (use a brand made with cocoa butter), finely chopped

Passion Fruit Sauce (recipe follows), for serving

Position rack in center of oven and preheat to 350°F. Lightly butter a 9-inch springform pan.

To make crust, combine vanilla wafer crumbs, butter and sugar in a medium bowl. Press evenly onto bottom of pan. Bake until lightly browned around edges, about 10 minutes. Reduce oven temperature to 325°F.

To make filling, heat heavy cream in a small saucepan over low heat. Remove from heat, add white chocolate and stir until melted. Cool slightly.

In a large bowl, beat cream cheese, eggs, sugar and vanilla with an electric mixer on high speed just until smooth, scraping down sides of bowl as needed. (A heavy-duty elec-tric mixer with the paddle blade works best.) Mix in melted white chocolate. Do not overbeat; too much air beaten into the batter is one cause of cracked cheesecake. Pour into pan and bake until sides are lightly puffed and beginning to brown (center will look unset), 40 to 45 minutes. Remove from oven. Run a thin, sharp knife around inner edge of pan to release cheesecake from sides of pan. Cool completely in pan on a wire cake rack.

Remove sides of pan. Wrap cheesecake in plastic wrap and refrigerate until chilled, at least 4 hours or overnight.

To make glaze, bring heavy cream to a simmer in a small saucepan over low heat. Remove from heat, add white choco-late and stir until melted. Unwrap cheesecake. Pour glaze over top of cheesecake and spread thinly. Refrigerate to set glaze, about 15 minutes. (The cheesecake can be made up to 2 days ahead, and then loosely covered with plastic wrap and refrig-erated.)

To serve, cut cake into wedges with a hot knife (dip into hot water between slices). Serve chilled, with Passion Fruit Sauce.

PASSION FRUIT SAUCE: Bring one 14-ounce package thawed frozen passion fruit juice (available at Latino mar-kets) and ½ cup sugar to a boil in a medium nonreactive saucepan. Dissolve 1 tablespoon cornstarch in ¼ cup water, and whisk into boiling juice. Cook until thickened. Transfer to a covered container and cool. Cover and refrigerate until serving. (The sauce can be made 2 days ahead, and then cooled, covered and refrigerated.) Makes 1¾ cups sauce.

Acknowledgments

The siege of 710 started on January 4, 2005, and ended some eight weeks later. If style is grace under pressure, then Lilly is style and graciousness personified. First thanks to her always for her enthusiasm, support, creativity and, oh, those meals!

Second thanks go to Jim Bradbeer, Scott Beaumont, Sandi Davidson and their terrific team at Sugartown. To single anyone out is doing someone else an injustice, so thanks to all but a little extra thanks to Kate Kenny, Whitney Hardy, Pat Borjeson, Courtney Reagan and Darlene Brinker.

There's a remarkable crew of people who joined forces to bring this book about. There is Nick Wollner, of 1919, who produced the book and shepherded us from start to finish, and Alison Lew, who magically put the elements—text, photos and illustrations—together to create something as visually delicious as one of Lilly's culinary treats. Rick Rodgers did a great job translating Lilly's "some of this and a handful of that" menus into easy-to-follow recipes. Ben Fink captured perfect moments with his camera lens, and Izak Zenou caught the Lilly spirit and turned it into whimsical illustrations. William Smith prepared all the glorious food under a crazy schedule—Thanksgiving in the morning and Fourth of July in the afternoon. Joe Maer's work as a stylist resulted in sumptuous vignettes. Last, but hardly least, John Silbersack is the superglue who held us together.

Tibby Bartram, Jeff Kavanaugh, Alex Ritterbush, Rachel Rheingold and Matthew Vohr were all participants in the siege of 710 and offered invaluable help, along with Gary Philo, who was left behind to hold down the fort.

Lilly's family—nuclear and extended—went out of their way to be helpful and to all of them goes a big thank-you: Peter and Amy Pulitzer, Liza Pulitzer and her son Bobby Leidy, Minnie and Kevin McKluskey and their children, Lilly and Rodman Leas and Jack McCluskey, Flo Chase, Maud Symington, Lilly and Barry Van Gerbig, Jessie Pulitzer, Kai Pulitzer, Mac and Kourtney Pulitzer, MacLean Pulitzer Jr. and Zac and Nikki Pulitzer.

Then there are her "peeps," those lucky devils who, over the years, have celebrated many a holiday at Lilly's. Their memories were so helpful. Thanks to Jerry Beebe, Eloise Cuddeback, Susanna Cutts, Franci Dixon, Peter Duchin, Ellen Gilbertson, Mark Gilbertson, Glee, Mercedes and Steve Gotwald, Nancy "Na-Na" Kezele, Bob Leidy, Julie McConnell and Betty Navarro.

In Palm Beach, additional thanks go to Theresa Moschetta Beresford, Kelly Garvey, Wayne Hosford, Sasha Lickle, Sten Lilja, Addison Linck, Robbie Linck, Brooke Raich, Courtney Ritterbush, Burke Ross, Wap Smit, Feliciana Tello, Esperanze Ulloa and her daughter Mercedes, and Luz Ulloa.

We'd like to give special thanks to the following companies for their generosity and support in making the project possible: Bernardaud, Michael C. Fina, Lenox, Norcross Patio, Tupperware, Uncommon Goods, Vanderpool & McCoy Linens, Villeroy & Boch and Waterford.

We wouldn't be celebrating colorful holidays if it weren't for the help of these fine folk: Slim Aarons, Jonathan Beckerman, Kathie Berlin, Paula and Bob Cashin, Colleen and Matthew Cohen, Dick Duane and Bob Thixton, Dominick Dunne, Ari Fridkis, Doris Kearns Goodwin, never mind Sally Kilbridge and Bob Payne, Betty Kuhner, Kate Kuhner, Gary Langstaff, Patrick McBride, David McGoldrick, Victoria Moran, Katy Mulvaney, Kathy Orrico, Matte Osian, Kathrin Seitz, Charles Spicer, Jeff Steele, Dek and Kathleen Tillett, Casey and Keith Warman, Maura Buckley Wollner and John and Laura Worth.

Working with Harper Collins is a wonderful experience, and for that thanks go to Joe Tessitore, Libby Jordan, Diane Aronson, Leah Carlson Stanisic, Jennifer Hirshlag, Karen Lumley, Jessica Peskay, Donna Ruvituso, Ryu Spaeth and Meegan Spellman, with extra thanks to Shelby Meizlik. Kathy Huck is, has been and hopefully will continue to be our guardian angel, as well as being a talented, supportive and delightful-to-work-with editor.

As ever, best love to Meghan, Colleen and Kevin.

—JAY MULVANEY

Recipe Index